FROM

GENERATION

TO

GENERATION

Reaching, Raising Up and Releasing
Every Next Generation

BAYLESS CONLEY

Answers Press

From Generation to Generation
Reaching, Raising Up and Releasing Every Next Generation

Copyright © 2016 by Bayless Conley

First Edition 2016

Answers with Bayless Conley
PO Box 417
Los Alamitos, CA 90720

ISBN: 978-1-942464-21-1

Printed in Germany

CONTENTS

One generation shall praise Your works to another, and shall declare Your mighty acts.

— Psalm 145:4

INTRODUCTION

One of the greatest burdens on my heart is to successfully *reach*, *raise up*, and *release* the next generation. To see them solidly planted in God's house where they can flourish as they serve the Lord alongside those of an older generation, pursuing God's plans and engaging the world with the glorious news of the Gospel—together.

And I'm not alone in this. Almost everywhere I travel in the world, pastors and church leaders are acutely aware of the need to build bridges to, and work together with, those younger than themselves.

We must think and act generationally.

This is not an option if we are going to see the purposes of God fulfilled in our churches and through our lives. God's design is for the generations to be connected, serving the Lord together, using the strengths of each to impact the world for Christ.

In the following pages, I outline the role, responsibility, and opportunity that each generation has to support, encourage, strengthen, and build up one another so that together we can reach our world with the Good News of Jesus Christ… while ensuring that the coming generations are empowered and equipped to do the same.

The TAKE ACTION section at the end of each chapter can be done alone or in a group setting. Putting the principles we learn into action is the difference between being fruitful and forgetful (James 1:22-25). Following are some thoughts to consider before you embark on the TAKE ACTION sections of this book.

Meditation

Take time to digest what you have read. Think about the Points to Ponder along with anything else that stood out to you in the chapter. Take time to write down your thoughts. Someone wisely once said: *"Taking notes helps to crystallize thoughts and promote action."*

Our Final Authority—God's Word

His Word is forever settled in heaven; we need to let it be forever settled as our final authority on all matters of life and faith (Psalm 119:89, 128).

Fill in the blanks, finishing the Scriptures that are referenced in the TAKE ACTION section (all of the referenced Scriptures can be found in the corresponding chapter).

Application

This segment of the TAKE ACTION section will help bring things into focus and stimulate you to consider practical ways the message can apply to and be implemented by you.

Your written responses may be as simple as "pray for the youth of our church five minutes a day," or as detailed as coming up with a blueprint for a mentoring program.

Simple or detailed, the point is to get you to put your thoughts on paper in order to help move you (or your group) towards some kind of action.

Group Discussion

For by wise counsel you can wage your war, and in an abundance of counselors there is victory and safety. (Proverbs 24:6 AMP)

Be willing to share your thoughts and insights, and be willing to listen to and consider the thoughts and insights of others. One of the beautiful things about the Church is that we are indeed a body, which is dependent upon all of the parts supplying what they are supposed to supply (Ephesians 4:16).

Ask questions. If you are seeking clarity regarding a statement or concept in the chapter, ask the group what they think. Dialogue, listen, explore. Do your best to discern what the Holy Spirit is saying to you personally, and to the group as a whole (Acts 15:28).

Questions to Get You Started

The "questions to get you started" are just that, starting points for your discussion. Use them to begin if you feel they will be helpful, but make sure you ask the questions and discuss the things that are resonating in your heart most strongly.

Game Plan

This is the time when you write down and commit to implement some specific steps of action. It's all right to start small, so long as you start. May the Lord direct your steps and give you much fruit for His glory.

Prayer

Ask for God's guidance and blessing as you move out and become a doer of His Word.

CHAPTER ONE
PASSING THE BATON

Have you ever wondered why God chose Abraham to be the father of the chosen people and why, through him and his descendants, the Savior of the world would eventually come? Why not choose a Pacific Islander or a European or an African or Indian or Asian? Why did God select this solitary figure from the Middle East living in Ur of the Chaldeans? The Scriptures give us only one answer to these questions, and it is immensely illuminating.

Genesis 18:17-19,

> *17 And the LORD said, Shall I hide from Abraham that thing which I do; 18 Seeing that Abraham shall surely become a great and mighty nation, and all the nations of the earth shall be blessed in him? 19 For I know him, that he will command his children and his household after him, and they shall keep the way of the LORD, to do justice and judgment; that the LORD may bring upon Abraham that which he hath spoken of him.* (KJV)

The phrase *"for I know him"* in verse 19 can be literally translated, "I have chosen him or singled him out." And why did God choose Abraham? God is clear. The one reason was this: *"He will command his children and his household after him, and they shall keep the way of the LORD, to do justice and judgment."*

God knew Abraham *would be generationally minded*, that he would successfully transmit what he had learned and train the following generations to follow God and His ways!

YOU AND I MUST BE COMMITTED TO A GENERATIONAL TRANSMISSION OF TRUTH, HISTORY, AND THE REALITY OF GOD.

If that was the single revealed reason God chose Abraham—through whom the entire world would be blessed—that should speak volumes to our hearts as to why thinking and acting generationally is so important to us today.

I believe that single passage alone would be enough to make the case for thinking generationally, but Scripture is replete with passages that point us to the importance of generational thinking. Let me show you just how important this is to God, starting with King David.

King David and the Generations

Psalm 71:17-18,

> [17] *O God, you have taught me from my earliest childhood, and I have constantly told others about the wonderful things you do.* [18] *Now that I am old and gray, do not abandon me, O God. Let me proclaim your power to this new generation, your mighty miracles to all who come after me.* (NLT)

King David was very generationally minded. He prayed for sufficient strength to transmit what he knew of God to those coming after him. But David's words reflect more than just his personal desire or feelings. In praying such a prayer, he was aligning himself perfectly with what God was desiring for his life… and by implication, for yours and mine.

The thought is expressed even more forcefully in Psalm 78:1-7,

> [1] *O my people, hear my teaching;*
> *listen to the words of my mouth.*
> [2] *I will open my mouth in parables,*
> *I will utter hidden things, things from of old—*
> [3] *what we have heard and known,*
> *what our fathers have told us.*
> [4] *We will not hide them from their children;*
> *we will tell the next generation*
> *the praiseworthy deeds of the LORD,*
> *his power, and the wonders he has done.*
> [5] *He decreed statutes for Jacob*
> *and established the law in Israel,*
> *which he commanded our forefathers*
> *to teach their children,*
> [6] *so the next generation would know them,*
> *even the children yet to be born,*
> *and they in turn would tell their children.*
> [7] *Then they would put their trust in God*
> *and would not forget his deeds*
> *but would keep his commands.* (NIV)

Notice in verse 5 that God *commanded* His people to transmit truth generationally. It was not optional for His people then, and it is not optional for us, as His people, today. If we are to walk in obedience to our Lord, we must make teaching and raising up the next generation in the ways of God a priority. If we do, the next generation will know Him and trust Him.

This mandate is reinforced by Psalm 79:13,

> *Then we your people, the sheep of your pasture, will praise you forever; from generation to generation we will recount your praise.* (NIV)

If you count yourself as one of God's people and one of His sheep, this is for you. You and I must be committed to a generational transmission of truth, history, and the reality of God.

A Generational Hall of Fame

Hebrews chapter 11 has been called by some the "faith hall of fame." In it, we find a long list of men and women who did exploits for God, trusting Him when faced with seemingly insurmountable obstacles and impossible situations. As I was rereading this amazing chapter one day, something dawned on me. *All of these heroes and heroines of faith are set out sequentially and generationally.*

Notice that the writer begins by naming people individually like Abel, Enoch, Abraham, Sarah, Joseph, Moses, and Rahab. Then he begins to group them by periods of history such as Gideon, Barak, Samson, and Jephthah, who were all from the time of the Judges. This generational list flows right into chapter 12 where it brings out a powerful truth concerning the race we must run (or the work we must accomplish) for Christ. Hebrews 12:1 sums up chapter 11 this way,

> *Therefore we also, since we are surrounded by so great a cloud of witnesses, let us lay aside every weight, and the sin which so easily ensnares us, and let us run with endurance the race that is set before us.*

As the writer of Hebrews sums up chapter 11, he uses an analogy from the ancient Olympic Games in his encouragement to believers. In fact, even the statement regarding the great cloud of witnesses is a reference to the games. When a spectator was seated in the upper seats, near the top of a stadium, it was referred to as being seated "in the clouds."[1] (I was raised referring to such seats as being in the "nosebleed section"!)

The picture the writer is painting is that of faithful saints who, after having served God in their generation, are now actively cheering us on as we continue the race. The idea is that the race is not yet finished. We are still engaged in the same race they were running, as the race is successive! Each generation completes their lap, but that doesn't end the race. Instead, each generation hands off the baton to the next. And for us, it is now our turn as the baton has been passed to us. The race of faith is a relay race!

Jesus put it succinctly when He spoke to His disciples about their ministry in John 4:38. He told them, *"Others have labored, and you have entered into their labors."*

Running Together

Now, I realize that whenever the example of a generational relay race is used and the "passing of the baton" is mentioned, some older church members begin to get a bit nervous. To them, "passing the baton" is the equivalent of the younger generation saying, "You've had your turn; now it's ours, so please step aside and don't get in our way." They fear they are being put out to pasture and the race is no longer theirs to run.

---

[1] Renner, Rick. "February 17—A Great Cloud of Witnesses." *Sparkling Gems from the Greek: 365 Greek Word Studies for Every Day of the Year to Sharpen Your Understanding of God's Word.* Tulsa, OK: Teach All Nations, 2003. 98. Print.

BUT THAT IS NOT WHAT A GENERATIONAL TRANSFER LOOKS LIKE AT ALL!

Generational transfer is not about pushing aside those who have paved the way, borne the burden and heat of the day... and financed everything. It is not about asking them to suddenly step out of the way and fade into obscurity and inactivity.

It is about running together.

Imagine if you would, those few moments where one runner, nearing the end of his part in the relay, strains while holding out the baton to his teammate ahead. Slow the whole scene down in your mind and look at it closely. Both men are running together. Both are moving in the same direction. Both have their hand on the baton. Their strides are in harmony with each other.

THEY MUST BE INTRODUCED TO HIS POWER! That scene—where the baton is being passed—while occurring in only a few seconds on the track, takes decades spiritually. It is something you and I must be engaged in for the remainder of our time on earth! It is the members of God's family, young and old, running together and serving together.

Malachi said it well in Malachi 4:6, when he prophesied regarding the ministry of John the Baptist as he prepared the way for Christ,

> *"He will turn the hearts of the fathers to the children,*
> *And the hearts of the children to their fathers..."*

This verse should literally read, "He will turn the hearts of the fathers **with** the children," meaning that the hearts of both generations will be turned to God together... worshiping together, serving together, running their race together.

So Scripture not only speaks to the importance of investing in, teaching, and raising up the next generation to follow after God, but it is also explicit on how we are to run *together* in reaching our world for Christ.

God's view of the importance of the generations working together, even to the end of days, is captured by Peter as he quotes Joel's prophecy on the day of Pentecost in Acts 2:17,

> *"And it shall come to pass in the last days, says God,*
> *That I will pour out of My Spirit on all flesh;*
> *Your sons and your daughters shall prophesy,*
> *Your young men shall see visions,*
> *Your old men shall dream dreams."*

This promise speaks of three generations: Sons and daughters, young men, and old men. Three generations all experiencing the outpouring and empowerment of the Holy Spirit and His gifts together for one purpose… to bring in an end-time harvest of souls together. As Acts 2:21 tells us, the supreme purpose for the outpouring of God's Spirit is so that, *"whoever calls on the name of the LORD shall be saved."*

They Dropped the Baton

Running together to ensure a smooth handing of the baton to the next generation is not automatic. It is something we have to do with great intentionality. In fact, there are several scriptural examples where proper priority wasn't given to this, and the baton was dropped between generations. And, as we will see, the results were disastrous.

The first example is found in Judges 2:7-12. Here's what it says,

⁷ So the people served the LORD all the days of Joshua, and all the days of the elders who outlived Joshua, who had seen all the great works of the LORD which He had done for Israel. ⁸ Now Joshua the son of Nun, the servant of the LORD, died when he was one hundred and ten years old. ⁹ And they buried him within the border of his inheritance at Timnath Heres, in the mountains of Ephraim, on the north side of Mount Gaash. ¹⁰ When all that generation had been gathered to their fathers, another generation arose after them who did not know the LORD nor the work which He had done for Israel.

¹¹ Then the children of Israel did evil in the sight of the LORD, and served the Baals; ¹² and they forsook the LORD God of their fathers, who had brought them out of the land of Egypt; and they followed other gods from among the gods of the people who were all around them, and they bowed down to them; and they provoked the LORD to anger.

Joshua was an outstanding leader for his generation. He was used by God in amazing ways to bring the nation of Israel into the Promised Land. But there was one glaring failure. He and his contemporaries failed to make the handoff to those coming after them.

Verse 7 states that all those who had seen and experienced the supernatural power of God at work served the Lord. Apparently, the next generation had not been taught about those experiences, nor had they encountered God's supernatural work in their midst. There was a failure to raise up the next generation to know and fear God, and they were never made acquainted with His mighty acts. Consequently, the commentary on the next generation is actually an indictment against both generations.

Not Enough

The church of today seems to believe that the way to influence and impact the next generation is through technology and creative human expression. In fact, we pride ourselves in being techno-savvy and artsy, but that is not enough! Light shows, cool music, and well-directed dramatic presentations are not sufficient to keep a young generation on track with God. They must be introduced to His power!

My own conversion was amidst a storm of healing and super-natural events. I witnessed and experienced the gifts of the Holy Spirit as well as solid preaching from God's Word. The people who helped bring me to Christ were not ashamed in any way of God's power and were quick to call upon Him in prayer when that power was needed.

Is it possible that one of the major reasons for the disconnect between generations in so many churches today is that there is no display of God's power in our midst? No evidence of His presence? May heaven help us to get back on our knees and cry out mightily for God's hand to move among us and through us as we continue to faithfully teach and preach His Word.

Your Sons Do Not Walk In Your Ways

Another example of a failure to effectively pass the spiritual baton to the next generation is Samuel. Samuel was one of Israel's outstanding leaders. As you read the account of his ministry, he seems "larger than life" in many ways. He possessed an astonishing personal relationship with God, was used in supernatural ways, and was reverenced by all. But somehow, he failed to pass the baton to his own sons.

First Samuel 8:1-5 is a very sad commentary,

> [1] *Now it came to pass when Samuel was old that he made his sons judges over Israel.* [2] *The name of his firstborn was Joel, and the name of his second, Abijah; they were judges in Beersheba.* [3] *But his sons did not walk in his ways; they turned aside after dishonest gain, took bribes, and perverted justice.*
>
> [4] *Then all the elders of Israel gathered together and came to Samuel at Ramah,* [5] *and said to him, "Look, you are old, and your sons do not walk in your ways. Now make us a king to judge us like all the nations."*

There is no reason for us to believe that Samuel making his sons judges was an act of nepotism. Everything we know from the divine record regarding Samuel would lead us to believe that his boys must have showed promise or had some positive spiritual fruit in their lives. It would have been quite inconsistent with Samuel's character to have placed them in such positions of authority otherwise.

It is possible that Joel and Abijah's descent into the world of bribery and dishonesty was entirely the result of their own wicked rebellion; Samuel having provided all the necessary instruction and leadership for their spiritual success. After all, look at Adam and Eve in the garden. God was the perfect parent, teacher, and companion, providing everything they needed for a blessed life;

yet by an act of their will, they discarded all of that and went down a destructive path. You certainly can't accuse God of doing a bad job in raising His kids!

Perhaps Samuel's sons were exclusively to blame for the disconnect with their father's ways. However, it is much more likely that Samuel failed to provide some necessary things in order to successfully pass the baton to his offspring. And because Samuel didn't transmit what he had to his own sons, Israel moved from a theocracy, where God was their King, to a monarchy, which radically affected their future as a nation.

Samuel, as a young child, had been brought to the temple by his mother Hannah. From that time on he lived with the priest Eli and his two sons, serving the Lord in the temple. There is an unmistakable parallel between the sons of Eli and the sons of Samuel. Eli's sons were engaged in the same sinful behavior (and worse) as Samuel's sons. Eli failed to successfully transmit what he had experienced and knew of God to his sons. Samuel, at least to some degree, seemed to repeat Eli's failed example of reaching and raising up those who were to follow him.

Transmitting What We Have

In view of Samuel's story, I want to turn your attention to Acts 3 where we find the story of the lame man who was healed. In this chapter, Peter makes an unforgettable statement to the lame man before ministering to him. He said, *"What I do have I give you"* (Acts 3:6).

We can only give away what we possess.

In considering Samuel's story as it relates to his sons carrying on in his footsteps, there is one thing that stands out in sharp relief among Samuel's attributes, which might have tipped the balance in his boys deciding which pathway to choose.

It begins with Samuel, as a boy, under tremendous peer pressure from Eli's sons. Eli's sons were rebellious, stealing temple offerings, bullying God's people, and committing sexual sin. Yet, Samuel remained pure, never following their constant negative example. The one distinguishing feature of Samuel's life during this season was his ability to discern the Holy Spirit's voice. It was a spiritual discipline that he learned through a process (see 1 Samuel 3). In fact, the first thing the Lord ever told Samuel was that He was going to judge Eli's house because of the wicked behavior of his sons and because Eli failed to do anything about it.

MAY HEAVEN HELP US TO GET BACK ON OUR KNEES.

It seems that the greatest factor in keeping Samuel on the right path, especially during this critical time of his life, was listening to God's voice. While Samuel might not have had every skill, strength, or insight to pass on to his own sons, he did have this one thing… the ability to discern and listen to God's voice. One wonders, "Samuel, did you pass this on to your sons? Did you instruct them at all along these lines? If it kept you, wouldn't it have kept them?"

Squirrels Again?

When our son Harrison was still very small, I spent time teaching him how to pray—both speaking and *listening* to God. We would kneel down together next to his bed and talk to God. We praised and made our requests, and then we would get quiet and listen. I always told him that prayer is a dialogue, a two-way street where both we and God communicate, and that whatever God has to say is far more important than anything we have to say. I encouraged him to listen in his heart for God's answers, or instructions, or even the faintest impressions the Holy Spirit might give.

One night as we were kneeling together, having just prayed for a number of people and things, I said, "Son, let's ask God if there is anyone or anything else He wants us to pray for. If anything comes into our hearts after we ask, we will pray."

We knelt quietly for a few minutes, and I soon could tell that Harrison had something he thought we should pray for. "What is it, son?" I asked. "I feel like God wants us to pray for the squirrels," he responded. So, we prayed for the squirrels, that they would be warm and have enough nuts for the winter.

The following evening we were praying again and, once more, we quietly waited for any "prayer instructions" in our hearts. I watched the funniest expression come over my son's face as he knelt there with his eyes closed. He suddenly said out loud (to God, I think), "Squirrels again?!" After I finished laughing, we prayed once again for the squirrels!

The point of this story is passing on what we know. Yes, Harrison was learning to listen for God's voice in prayer, and it wasn't long before he was distinguishing between what was a genuine Holy Spirit prompting and what was not.

When Samuel was starting out, he was unacquainted with God's voice and had to learn to discern it as well. What might have happened if Samuel had helped train his own sons to listen for and obey God's voice? Perhaps the baton wouldn't have been dropped, his sons would have stayed on track, and Israel might not have rejected God as their Sovereign.

It is imperative for us to connect with the next generation and pass on the truth we know.

At Least There Will Be Peace and Truth in My Days

Another glaring example of the generational baton being fumbled was in the case of Hezekiah, one of Judah's greatest kings. This story is found in 2 Kings 20:16-19,

> [16] *Then Isaiah said to Hezekiah, "Hear the word of the LORD:* [17] *'Behold, the days are coming when all that is in your house, and what your fathers have accumulated until this day, shall be carried to Babylon; nothing shall be left,' says the LORD.* [18] *And they shall take away some of your sons who will descend from you, whom you will beget; and they shall be eunuchs in the palace of the king of Babylon.'"*
>
> [19] *So Hezekiah said to Isaiah, "The word of the LORD which you have spoken is good!" For he said, "Will there not be peace and truth at least in my days?"*

While Hezekiah is acclaimed as a great king, he built no bridges with the coming generation. When he was told that some of his descendants—the next generation—would be carried away into Babylon, his response was self-centered and short-sighted, "At least there will be peace and truth in my days." Clearly, he was only concerned for himself and felt that when the time came, his sons could sort things out for themselves. What a terrible, myopic attitude, with the consequence that Babylon did become the undoing of the kingdom of Judah, and his sons were taken into captivity.

Many in the church today embrace similar attitudes: "As long as I'm blessed, have peace (freedom from my troubles), and have truth (get to hear good preaching), that's great! The next generation can sort out their problems. That's not my responsibility." The result of that type of mind-set will be the same today as it was in Hezekiah's day—captivity in Babylon.

IT TAKES WILLINGNESS AND PATIENCE ON BOTH SIDES TO EFFECTIVELY PASS THE BATON.

By the time of the New Testament, Babylon no longer existed as a nation. But it is referred to, particularly in the book of Revelation. Babylon came to be known as an emblem of worldliness, corruption, and lust. The truth is, if we don't successfully build bridges connecting the generations, the world will capture many of our sons and daughters! They will end up being a spiritually bankrupt generation in captivity to sin and the devil.

They Didn't Sort It Out

Hezekiah left his sons to sort out the future on their own. But they didn't sort it out. To say that the events that followed were disastrous would be an understatement. Take a moment to read the sad record of what came to pass directly on the heels of Hezekiah's reign, as recorded in 2 Kings 20:21; 21:1-6, 16.

> [21] *So Hezekiah rested with his fathers. Then Manasseh his son reigned in his place.* [1] *Manasseh was twelve years old when he became king, and he*

27

reigned fifty-five years in Jerusalem. His mother's name was Hephzibah. ² And he did evil in the sight of the LORD, according to the abominations of the nations whom the LORD had cast out before the children of Israel. ³ For he rebuilt the high places which Hezekiah his father had destroyed; he raised up altars for Baal, and made a wooden image, as Ahab king of Israel had done; and he worshiped all the host of heaven and served them. ⁴ He also built altars in the house of the LORD, of which the LORD had said, "In Jerusalem I will put My name." ⁵ And he built altars for all the host of heaven in the two courts of the house of the LORD. ⁶ Also he made his son pass through the fire, practiced soothsaying, used witchcraft, and consulted spiritists and mediums. He did much evil in the sight of the LORD, to provoke Him to anger.... ¹⁶ Moreover Manasseh shed very much innocent blood, till he had filled Jerusalem from one end to another, besides his sin by which he made Judah sin, in doing evil in the sight of the LORD.

Why did Hezekiah have such an attitude? Where did it come from? It probably arose from the fact that he had no mentor himself. His father Ahaz had been a wicked king and an idolater. Hezekiah had to discover and build a relationship with God all on his own. It was the only model he knew. He had no other pattern; he had no spiritual father to guide him. So he figured if he could "work it out," his sons could do the same. Unfortunately, it didn't turn out that way.

Perhaps you are a first-generation Christian like me. I never heard the Gospel until I was in my twenties, and I have never really had a spiritual father who took me under his wing and instructed me. But I refuse to make those coming after me learn it all on their own. How about you? Let's make a conscious effort to reach, raise up, and release those coming after us, imparting what we know, putting the baton firmly in their hand.

He Rejected the Advice of the Elders

When there is a disconnect generationally and the baton is dropped, we cannot always lay the blame at the older generation's feet. Sometimes, it is the younger generation that refuses the handoff. King Rehoboam, the son of Solomon, illustrates this point well (see 1 Kings 12 and 2 Chronicles 10).

Once young Rehoboam replaced his father as king, the nation gathered before him to make a request to lighten some of the intolerable burdens that Solomon had placed upon them. You see, in his later years, King Solomon had backslidden, and among other things, he made life very difficult for many in Israel. Rehoboam told them to return in three days for his answer.

First, he asked counsel of the elders—the leaders from the older generation—about how they thought he should answer the people. They basically said he should yield to their request and deal kindly with the people, thus forging their support and loyalty. Then he asked the opinion of the young men with whom he had grown up. They told him to be harsh with the people and tell them that his little finger was thicker than his father's waist, meaning he would add to their burdens.

Rehoboam rejected the counsel of the elders, effectively batting away the baton they were trying to hand to him. When the three days were up, he answered according to the counsel the young men had given him. The result of this generational disconnect was that ten of Israel's tribes walked out—permanently! The nation was divided from that day forward. Ten tribes formed Israel, making their capital in Samaria, while the other two tribes (Judah and Benjamin) became known as Judah, making their capital in Jerusalem. Years of mistrust and bloodshed followed, all because one generation refused to listen to another.

It Must Go Both Ways

It takes willingness and patience on both sides to effectively pass the baton, bringing the strengths of different generations together. Without a voluntary effort of young and old to come together, we will never finish *our* race the way we are destined to finish.

Those from the younger generation need to listen to and respect the wisdom of the older generation, consciously connecting, receiving, and being an active part of the life of the local church. *Even if everything we do is not cool or trendy*. And the older generation needs to open up and share, be patient, and *be willing to accept change*.

Personal preference in musical style is a classic example. Following is a portion of a letter written to the leadership of a church regarding a new song that had been introduced.

> *I am no music scholar, but I feel I know appropriate church music when I hear it. Last Sunday's new hymn—if you can call it that—sounded like a sentimental love ballad one would expect to hear crooned in a saloon. If you insist on exposing us to rubbish like this—in God's house!—don't be surprised*

if many of the faithful look for a new place to worship.
The hymns we grew up with are all we need.

This letter was written in 1863, and the song they were concerned about was the hymn "Just As I Am."[2]

Another letter said,

What is wrong with the inspiring hymns with which we grew up? When I go to church, it is to worship God, not to be distracted with learning a new hymn. Last Sunday's was particularly unnerving. The tune was un-singable and the new harmonies were quite distorting.

This letter was written in 1890 about the hymn "What a Friend We Have in Jesus."[3]

I recently spoke to a friend who is the music director of one of the largest churches in the United Kingdom. He told me of a number of very old letters that someone had shared with him about church music. Some of these letters had been written in the 1800s and some in the early 1900s. They said things like: *"The music is too loud. It's too lively. It will never catch on."* And, *"It's not in keeping with the tradition of the church."* These statements made by church members were about the songs "Amazing Grace," "Be Thou My Vision," and "Power in the Blood."

THE PRICE OF DROPPING THE BATON IS FAR TOO HIGH.

It seems that things haven't changed much with some people in church! Many of the people today who cherish these songs,

---

[2, 3] Kimball, Dan. "The Controversial Organ." *Dan Kimball: Vintage Faith*, n.p., 2 July 2008. Web. 06 May 2015.

that were so strongly opposed when they were first introduced, are saying the same things about some of the new music in the church today. Expecting and embracing change in some things (like musical style) is essential if God's people from different generations are going to serve together.

When I was first saved, I began attending a small Pentecostal church affectionately known as "The Tab" (short for Tabernacle). The members of The Tab were, for the most part, much older than me… way older than me. The songs we sang were not even close to the style of music I personally liked. Everyone clapped on one and three (instead of on two and four), and it appeared to me that God did not allow rhythm in church or for anyone to play more than the same three chords over and over. But if those were the rules, I was in! I sang with all my heart and wept regularly when we sang about Jesus and salvation.

Then, one day, I heard a song by the Talbot Brothers. I had known of them, before I was a Christian, through their band Mason Proffit. Apparently, they had become believers and were now singing about Jesus… but they were singing and playing in a style I was familiar with and liked! I remember thinking to myself, *This is allowable?!! Fantastic!!!* Young people actually expressing their faith in God through a contemporary music style. It was amazing and very liberating for me.

Our attitude should be, "Wow! Young people expressing their faith and worship to God in a musical style they can relate to, marvelous! It may not be my personal preference in musical style, but they are praising Jesus and singing God's Word. And I am going to encourage them and embrace them and thank the Lord that they are in His house!"

The person who says, "I don't like the music, so I'm going to find another church," has lost the plot. *If we don't learn to change, we will lose a generation!*

But the younger generation has to realize as well, that it is not all about them and what they can relate to. It is wrong for young people to, in essence, hold the church hostage and say: "We're not coming along if everything doesn't sound like us and look like us." The young people in God's family need to do some yielding and embracing as well.

A Successful Transition

Years ago, I heard of a quote by Charles Spurgeon. When asked what he was doing about the coming generation, he referred to Acts 13:36 where it states, *"For David, after he had served his own generation by the will of God, fell asleep."* He basically said he was, like David, serving his own generation, and the next would have to work things out for themselves. It was a very clever response, but one that I feel is unscriptural.

As we have already read, David was very generationally minded. He spoke several times in the Psalms of reaching the coming generations. In fact, the biblical record tells us that David did everything he could to prepare for Solomon and the coming generation (see 1 Chronicles 28–29).

David prepared wealth, resources, building materials, workers, and a leadership team to help Solomon. He also prayed for his son, encouraged him, and instructed him in the Word of God. And very importantly, he modeled humble leadership before him.

A successful transition was made, the baton was passed, and the kingdom was established in Solomon's hand.

I believe the Church today can do the same, by God's grace. We may inadvertently "color out of the lines" a bit while we are working on the picture—we are sure to make our share of mistakes—but we *MUST* succeed in this.

The price of dropping the baton is far too high.

A Prayer

Heavenly Father, we realize what must be done. It is Your plan that all of the generations work together in Your Kingdom. We will be active participants in bringing this to pass. We realize that in doing so, we need to lay down many of our personal preferences for the sake of Your Kingdom, and we do so willingly. Help us to connect with those both younger and older than us. We choose to be pliable, embracing change wherever it is needed. We choose to be open and respectful, doing all we can to encourage a generational connection in our church—even if it means that our age group is required to make the most changes. Forgive us for where we have failed in the past, and grant us success as we pursue Your desire for all the generations in Your house worshiping and working together as we bring a living Jesus to a dying world. Amen.

TAKE ACTION

CHAPTER ONE

Meditation

I will also meditate on all Your work, and talk of Your deeds. (Psalm 77:12)

Points to Ponder

1. God selected Abraham to be the father of the chosen people because He knew that Abraham would think and act generationally.

2. *Passing the baton* from an older generation to a younger one does not mean "getting out of the way" so the young men and women can have their turn. It is about running together.

3. It is important to transmit the things of God that are strong in our lives to the coming generations.

Our Final Authority—God's Word

Therefore all Your precepts concerning all things I consider to be right... (Psalm 119:128)

Psalm 78:3-4 (NIV)

³ *What we have heard and known,* _____

_____ .

⁴ *We will not hide them from their children;* _____

_____

_____

_____

_____ .

Psalm 79:13 (NIV)

Then we your people, _____

_____ *will praise you forever;*

from _____ *to* _____

we will recount _____ .

Acts 2:17

"And it shall come to pass in the last days, says God, That I will

_____

_____ *; Your*

_____ *shall prophesy,*

Your _____ *shall see visions,*

Your _____ *shall dream dreams."*

Judges 2:7

So the people served the LORD all the days of Joshua, and all the

days of the elders who _____

who had _____

_____

_____.

Application

What portions of the chapter stood out to you? Why? In what ways might they apply to you?

In what ways could you act upon and implement some of the principles brought out in this chapter? (Write down your thoughts and ideas. Even if they are rough and incomplete at this point, they will help you gain clarity and focus, and hopefully move you toward action.)

Group Discussion

For by wise counsel you can wage your war, and in an abundance of counselors there is victory and safety. (Proverbs 24:6 AMP)

Share your thoughts and insights about the chapter. Ask others to share their thoughts as well, and do your best to listen carefully.

Questions to Get You Started

Q. What stood out to you the most from this chapter?

Q. We saw that the consequences of failing to *pass the baton* can be monumental. Do you believe that we have the responsibility to pray and personally act when it comes to reaching and working with younger and older generations? If so, why? If not, why not?

Q. Are there any things that are "strong in you" (specific things that you have learned about God and life) that you feel you need to transmit to a younger generation?

Q. What do you feel that the Holy Spirit is saying to you about what you have studied so far?

Game Plan

But be doers of the word, and not hearers only… (James 1:22)

Steps I will personally take to help connect the generations:

(This can be as simple as "making it a matter of prayer" or "taking someone to lunch." Think about it and come up with a starting place. Remember, mighty oaks grow from small acorns.)

1. _____

2. _____

3. _____

Prayer

Commit your works to the LORD, and your thoughts will be established. (Proverbs 16:3)

Talk to God about what you have discovered and discussed. Commit your plans to Him; humbly ask for guidance, clarity, and blessing as you move forward.

THREE DISTINCT GENERATIONS

W hen I was a boy, I distinctly remember being sharply reprimanded by an older relative because I tried to share my opinion in an "adult conversation." I was present, and I was allowed to listen; but I was not allowed to share my thoughts or feelings. I was later told, "Children are meant to be seen but not heard." Sadly, this seems to be the attitude of some of the older saints in the church regarding the younger generations.

A friend of mine, who has served as an evangelist for many years, was of the same opinion. He didn't feel that those from a younger generation had much of value to share. That all changed one night at a conference he was attending.

The man leading the service that night called for all those serving in full-time preaching ministry to come forward. My friend complied, coming forward with a large group of ministers who were also attending. Next, the man in charge called for the "prayer teams" to come forward to pray for the ministers. To his dismay, my friend found himself face to face with a smiling 18-year-old girl who was ready to pray for him. He thought to himself, *What a waste of time this will be!*

As if hearing his thoughts, the young lady said, "My, aren't you cynical," and then, through a gift of the Holy Spirit, she began to speak to him about his inward weariness and disappointments, his personal struggles, and a number of things that God alone was aware of. He began to sob. Then, as she laid hands on him and prayed, a mighty presence of God descended on him; and for the next hour, he lay on the floor weeping and talking to God. That encounter changed his life. It resurrected a ministry that was dying on the vine, and it helped renew a passion for God that had been lost somewhere amidst the many storms of life. It also changed his opinion about the younger generation's ability to contribute.

The God of Generations

Let's go back for a moment to Acts 2:16-17. What I want to point you to is how God is a God of generations.

In this passage, as Peter endeavored to explain to the gathered multitude the meaning of the outpouring of the Spirit that the disciples had just experienced, he quoted from Joel's prophecy. Among other things, he made it clear that the experience was destined for more than just one generation or age group.

> [16] *"But this is what was spoken by the prophet Joel:*
> [17] *'And it shall come to pass in the last days, says God, That I will pour out of My Spirit on all flesh; Your sons and your daughters shall prophesy, Your young men shall see visions, Your old men shall dream dreams.'"*

Notice that this promise speaks of three distinct generations all experiencing the outpouring of the Spirit together. First, it mentions sons and daughters being the youngest generation. Next, it mentions young men, and finally, it speaks of old men. These classifications represent the three generations that have major influence in the world today.

Sons and daughters comprise what are commonly referred to as the *Millennials* (from teens to early thirties). The young men category includes those commonly referred to as *Gen X* (from early thirties to early fifties). The third generation Peter refers to are the old men, which consists of everyone older than those previously mentioned (which includes, but is not limited to, those referred to today as *Baby Boomers*).

God is not just the God of some past generation or the God of some up-and-coming generation. He is the God of *generations.* The God of Abraham, Isaac, and Jacob—all at once and all together, being filled by and used by His Spirit. A generational church is not just a church that has a youth department and a children's department. It is a church where all the generations are serving and working *together.*

A friend of mine, Mal Fletcher, described a generational church this way: "It is where Abraham *resources* Isaac, and Isaac *releases* Jacob, and Jacob *reveres* Abraham."[4] I wholeheartedly agree with that description.

The apostle John in his writings also recognizes and instructs these same three generations. This is what he says in 1 John 2:12-14,

> [12] *I write to you, little children, because your sins are forgiven you for His name's sake.* [13] *I write to you, fathers, because you have known Him who is from the beginning. I write to you, young men, because you have overcome the wicked one. I write to you, little children, because you have known the Father.* [14] *I have written to you, fathers, because you have known Him who is from the beginning.*

[4] Fletcher, M. n.d., Ongoing conversations

*I have written to you, young men, because you are
strong, and the word of God abides in you, And you
have overcome the wicked one.*

Again, we have three distinct generations serving God together, growing together, and carrying out Kingdom business together. Truth, values, and vision being transmitted from one to another, while embracing the particular accents, gifts, and callings that God places on each new generation.

The way God intends His family to function is for us to learn from the previous generation; taking everything they have acquired and passed on; incorporating that into the things God teaches us personally; thus mingling the gifts, knowledge, and strengths of each. Then, we pass on all of that to the next generation.

GOD IS A GOD OF GENERATIONS.

It is wrong for a new generation to have to start over. There should never be an older generation saying, "We had to learn the hard way, so figure it out on your own," or a younger generation saying, "We don't need what you experienced and learned; we have something new."

Each generation will certainly have its unique challenges, and God may do some things for and with them that were unknown to the previous generation. *But to achieve what God is calling us to do and to have the maximum impact upon our world for Christ, we must include and build upon the former things.* Each generation inspiring, encouraging, informing, supporting, and praying for the next… with all of us doing exploits for God ***together***.

Heroes in Waiting

If every dream we have can come to pass in our lifetime, then we are dreaming far too small and we really haven't caught the heart of

God like we should. If our efforts only have a planned impact for our lifetime, then we have not begun to think or act generationally.

Let me give you an example of how I believe God wants us to think. The story is found in 1 Samuel 16, where we find the prophet Samuel mourning over Saul. He is **EACH GENERATION INSPIRING, ENCOURAGING, INFORMING, SUPPORTING, AND PRAYING FOR THE NEXT.** not just mourning over Saul's failure and God's rejection of him as king. It was not just a personal sadness because of his relationship with and love for Saul. Samuel is grieving over lost opportunities and unfulfilled dreams because Saul represented a generation that never stacked up to what Samuel hoped they would be.

God interrupts Samuel's grieving with a message that we need to consider. It is found in 1 Samuel 16:1,

> *Now the LORD said to Samuel, "How long will you mourn for Saul, seeing I have rejected him from reigning over Israel? Fill your horn with oil, and go; I am sending you to Jesse the Bethlehemite. For I have provided Myself a king among his sons."*

While Samuel was mourning over lost opportunities, God was already looking to future possibilities. God always has His heroes in waiting. He is preparing them out in the shepherd's field to rescue and guide a nation; or in an Egyptian prison for the saving of the known world; or in Babylonian captivity to interpret dreams, speak to kings, and change the destiny of nations.

In Samuel's case, God's hero was someone from the next generation, the shepherd boy David.

In this particular story, Samuel represents the *fathers* generation, Saul the *young men*, and David the *little children*... or what we would call the Millennials. In a prophetic sense, the Millennials are our Davids. We must engage them and involve them because we can influence the world by influencing them!

"A Glorious Future Which We Are Not Destined to See"

David Livingstone, as he sat alone in the African wilderness, wrote the following words in his diary:

> Future missionaries will see conversions follow every sermon. We prepare the way for them. May they not forget the pioneers who worked in the thick gloom with few cheering rays to cheer except such as flow from Faith in God's promises. We work for a glorious future which we are not destined to see. (November 11, 1853)[5]

That is the attitude we need to embrace. And again, it is not about fading into obscurity and inactivity while we watch those of a younger generation do exploits for God. It is about all of us working together for Kingdom goals. Each generation being visited by God and used by God. The Abraham, Isaac, and Jacob generations combining their strengths for the cause of Christ.

I believe, however, there is a call from above to give special attention to equipping the "Jacob" generation, those John refers to as *little children*. Those of us from the older generations must do all we can to help resource and prepare those younger than us. We must be willing to sow in order that they may reap.

---

[5] Hammond, Peter. "Livingstone's First Mission to Africa." *Livingstone 200*. Web. 26 Aug. 2015. <www.livingstone200.org/index.php/biographical-articles/83-livingstone-s-first-mission-to-africa>.

I believe that, in principle, Scripture bears this out. When you look at the book of 1 John, John—guided by the Holy Spirit— gives the lion's share of his instruction to those of the youngest generation. John only refers to and instructs the *fathers* and *young men* in verses 12 to 14 of chapter 2, but he repeatedly refers to and instructs the *little children* throughout his letter.

- 1 John 2:1—*My little children, these things I write to you, so that you may not sin. And if anyone sins, we have an Advocate with the Father, Jesus Christ the righteous.*

- 1 John 2:12—*I write to you, little children, because your sins are forgiven you for His name's sake.*

- 1 John 2:13—*I write to you, little children, because you have known the Father.*

- 1 John 2:18—*Little children, it is the last hour; and as you have heard that the Antichrist is coming, even now many antichrists have come, by which we know that it is the last hour.*

- 1 John 3:7—*Little children, let no one deceive you. He who practices righteousness is righteous, just as He is righteous.*

- 1 John 3:18—*My little children, let us not love in word or in tongue, but in deed and in truth.*

- 1 John 4:4—*You are of God, little children, and have overcome them, because He who is in you is greater than he who is in the world.*

- 1 John 5:21—*Little children, keep yourselves from idols. Amen.*

John gives this youngest generation particular attention as he instructs them regarding important truths such as:

- Forgiveness
- Being Spirit-led
- Avoiding deceivers
- Lifestyle reveals true spirituality
- Authority in Christ
- Keeping God first

It is important for us to embrace this scriptural emphasis on the younger generation and do all we can to help equip them for what God has uniquely called them to do. With our help, they will influence and impact every aspect of society, including evangelism and Gospel preaching, politics, entertainment and the arts, sports, business, technology, science, education, and finance, to name a few.

A Unique Generation

Let me take a moment to talk about the Millennial generation. This generation is different. They are unlike the previous generation in several significant ways. They are much more oriented to being "team players" in that they seem to grasp the need for collaboration in order to achieve things on a large scale.

They are more civic-minded and less cynical than the previous generation. They also tend to be much more global in their thinking, desiring to build things that will help change the world.

Like Gen X that came before them, they are very community-oriented; but unlike Gen X, whose "getting together" was more for nurture and friendship, the Millennials gather together to talk about how they can *do* something for the world. They embrace the team concept... including the fact that teams need leaders. I believe that we can play a significant role in developing those leaders and, in turn, change the world.

CHAPTER TWO

Meditation

But his delight is in the law of the LORD, and in His law he meditates day and night. (Psalm 1:2)

Points to Ponder

1. Both Peter (in quoting Joel's prophecy) and John refer to three distinct generations serving God together and experiencing the outpouring of the Spirit together.

2. It is not right for a new generation to have to "start over." God's plan is for us to pass on what we learn, while at the same time embracing the strengths and unique qualities of each generation.

3. If every dream we have can come to pass in our lifetime, we are dreaming too small and we have yet to catch the heart of God like we should.

Our Final Authority—God's Word

Forever, O LORD, Your word is settled in heaven. (Psalm 119:89)

Acts 2:17

> *"And it shall come to pass in the last days, says God, That I will*
>
> _____
>
> _____ *; Your*
>
> _____ *shall prophesy,*
>
> *Your* _____ *shall see visions,*
>
> *Your* _____ *shall dream dreams."*

1 John 2:12-13

> [12] *I write to you,* _____
>
> _____
>
> *for His name's sake,* [13] *I write to you,* _____ *,*
>
> _____
>
> *who is from the beginning, I write to you,* _____
>
> _____
>
> _____ *.*

I write to you, little children, _____

_____ .

1 Samuel 16:1

*Now the LORD said to Samuel, "*_____

_____ *, seeing I have rejected him*

from _____ *? Fill your horn*

with oil, and go; I am sending you to Jesse the Bethlehemite. For

I have provided Myself _____ *among his sons."*

1 John 4:4

You are of God, little children, and have _____

_____ *because* _____

is greater than he who _____ .

Application

What portions of the chapter stood out to you? Why? In what ways might they apply to you?

In what ways could you act upon and implement some of the principles brought out in this chapter? (Write down your thoughts and ideas. Even if they are rough and incomplete at this point, they will help you gain clarity and focus, and hopefully move you toward action.)

_____

_____

_____

_____

_____

_____

_____

_____

_____

_____

_____

_____

_____

Group Discussion

Then those who feared the LORD spoke to one another... (Malachi 3:16)

Share your thoughts and insights about the chapter. Ask others to share their thoughts as well, and do your best to listen carefully.

Questions to Get You Started

Q. What stood out to you the most from this chapter?

Q. Do you think Peter's quoting of Joel's prophecy, which clearly speaks of different generations experiencing the power of the Spirit, is significant? Why?

Q. Why do you think John wrote more to the "little children" than to any other generation?

Q. What do you think some common objections might be as we seek to connect the generations in our churches?

Q. Can you think of suggestions to help overcome or solve these objections?

Q. What do you feel the Holy Spirit is saying to you about what you have studied so far?

Game Plan

Jesus replied, "But even more blessed are all who hear the word of God and put it into practice." (Luke 11:28 NLT)

Steps I will personally take to help connect the generations:

1. _____

2. _____

3. _____

Prayer

"For everyone who asks receives…" (Matthew 7:8)

Talk to God about what you have discovered and discussed. Perhaps ask God to enlarge your vision and help you be a part of something so big and expansive that it cannot be done in your lifetime.

And remember, a big part of prayer is listening. Endeavor to be sensitive to His voice and His impressions.

CHAPTER THREE
TRAIL MARKERS IN THE WILDERNESS

From my days as a young man until today, I have spent a lot of time backpacking and camping in the wilderness. During the last few years, I have made a few trips with some of the young men from our church. One destination we hiked to was a small mountain lake hidden away in a valley deep in the Sierra Nevada Mountains of California.

There is no hiking trail to this lake (which will remain unnamed due to the amazing fishing… some secrets need to be kept!). In order to reach it, once you are off the main trail you must travel cross-country, climbing over logs, scrambling over boulders, and traipsing over steep, pine needle–covered hillsides for hours. It takes two days on the main trail just to get to the place where you're finally able to head down the hillside and take the multiple-hour trek to our secret lake.

The lake can be found on a topography map of the region, but, as I said, there is no existing trail to the lake. There **I CAN ASSURE YOU, THE PAYOFF IS WORTH IT.** is, however, a series of "trail markers" along the way. These trail markers consist of three small rocks stacked one on top of another. One has to search to find them, as they are spread out over the demanding terrain. (They are generally about fifty yards apart.) If you can find them and are willing to make the difficult hike down, the payoff is worth it—a pristine mountain lake filled with hungry trout, exquisite scenery, and solitude.

I realize that for some, the idea of raising up and releasing a generation is quite daunting, a bit like the long, difficult hike to our secret lake. But I can assure you, the payoff is worth it. Similarly, many young people may feel like the necessary hike to engage an older generation is too far or too hard. To them I would also say, the payoff is worth it. In fact, the youth of our day will not be able to accomplish their mission for God without the support of the older generations.

In this chapter I want to set out some specific trail markers to help both young and old make the journey to a multigenerational church, where Abraham resources Isaac, Isaac releases Jacob, and Jacob reveres Abraham.

TRAIL MARKERS FOR THE YOUNGER GENERATION

Trail Marker #1: Honor the Older Generation

The first trail marker for the younger generation is found in Deuteronomy 5:16,

> *"Honor your father and your mother, as the LORD your God has commanded you, that your days may be long, and that it may be well with you in the land which the LORD your God is giving you."*

This is referred to in Scripture as the first commandment with a promise. It was reiterated by Jesus on a number of occasions, as well as being quoted by Paul in Ephesians and Colossians. While it is obviously referring to the relationship of natural children with their parents, the principle could (and should) be applied to honoring anyone from an older generation.

This is clearly what we are taught from Leviticus 19:32, *"Show respect for old people and honor them. Reverently obey me; I am the LORD"* (GNT).

The heart that embraces an honoring attitude toward seniors brings blessing from God.

The word *honor*, as found in Scripture, literally means "to value or prize, to respect." And interestingly enough, it also means "to make weighty," signifying that the younger generation should consider the counsel and example of the older generation very carefully.

Any input from someone older (be it guidance, correction, encouragement, or comfort) should carry weight with a younger person. To treat the wisdom of an older person *lightly* is to dishonor them.

How Much He Had Learned

When children grow to be teenagers, they are notorious for thinking they know it all. Their parents, who have served as their examples and teachers since birth, have suddenly become "stupid" and completely out of touch. And unfortunately, many times the child no longer receives his or her parents' instruction.

Mark Twain is quoted as having said, "When I was a boy of 14, my father was so ignorant I could hardly stand to have the old man around. But when I got to be 21, I was astonished at how much the old man had learned in seven years."

Regrettably, many times we see a parallel in spiritual things. For this reason, we find a multitude of admonitions in Scripture that encourage us to heed the counsel of an older generation. Following are just a few examples:

[8] Listen, my child, to what your father teaches you. Don't neglect your mother's teaching. [9] What you learn from them will crown you with grace and clothe you with honor. (Proverbs 1:8-9 NLT)

[1] Listen, my sons, to a father's instruction; pay attention and gain understanding. [2] I give you sound learning, so do not forsake my teaching. (Proverbs 4:1-2 NIV)

A wise son heeds his father's instruction, but a scoffer does not listen to rebuke. (Proverbs 13:1)

Listen to your father who begot you, and do not despise your mother when she is old. (Proverbs 23:22)

Trail Marker #2: Practice the Truth That You Hear

In chapter 2, I gave a list of the expansive instruction given to the *little children* generation in the book of 1 John. It is important to connect those admonitions to the statements John made to the same generation in 2 John and 3 John:

> *I rejoiced greatly that I have found some of your children walking in truth, as we received commandment from the Father. (2 John 1:4)*

> *I have no greater joy than to hear that my children walk in truth. (3 John 1:4)*

Notice that he didn't say he rejoiced because the children *listened* to truth, but because they *walked* in it. Walking denotes action. It means to practice or participate in. The truth must go beyond your ears and get into your feet!

I'm Not Leaving until You Baptize Me

Shortly after I was saved, I began attending a small Pentecostal church in town. I had come from a background of drug abuse and wild living, and, in many respects, I stood out among the congregation. Most of those attending were quite old and from very conservative backgrounds. I had long hair, and it was obvious to everyone that I was different.

I was living in a single room above a bar, and on a Friday night about 10 p.m., I was praying. I said to the Lord, *Help me draw closer to You. I want to know You more.* I felt like the Holy Spirit whispered to my heart, *I want you to get baptized.*

THE YOUNGER GENERATION SHOULD CONSIDER THE COUNSEL AND EXAMPLE OF THE OLDER GENERATION VERY CAREFULLY.

I immediately grabbed a towel, rolled it up, put it under my arm, and headed downstairs. I crossed the street to a phone booth and looked up the pastor's number. I called and told him I wanted to get baptized. "Who are you?" he asked.

"My name is Bayless," I responded. No recognition. "I'm the guy with long hair in your church." (I was the only one fitting that description.)

"Oh," he said. "Well, come on Sunday and we'll baptize you."

I was devastated. I was ready right then. After all, I'd heard the pastor say to the church, "If you want to get baptized, day or night, we'll do it." I had no idea he was just "preachin'" and really didn't mean it.

I came on Sunday, towel in hand, only to find they hadn't filled the baptismal tank. "Come back on Wednesday," the pastor told me. "We'll try and do it then."

But I refused to leave. "I need to be baptized," I pleaded.

He looked me up and down and said, "You *really* want to be baptized, don't you?"

"Yes," I said, thinking, *I wonder if it's this hard for everyone?* I had to force them to baptize me!

What is my point in sharing this piece of my history? I want the young person reading this to know we're not just "preachin'" when we share the truth of God that we have learned. We expect you to do more than listen; we expect you to act. Put what you hear into practice and cause some rejoicing in the older generation.

Trail Marker #3: Make Your Life an Example to Others

In writing to his young disciple Timothy, Paul exhorts him in 1 Timothy 4:12-14,

> [12] *Let no one despise your youth, but be an example to the believers in word, in conduct, in love, in spirit, in faith, in purity.* [13] *Till I come, give attention to reading, to exhortation, to doctrine.* [14] *Do not neglect the gift that is in you, which was given to you by prophecy with the laying on of the hands of the eldership.*

Even though you may be young and in a major learning stage in your life, you are still an example to someone. Someone is always watching!

The word translated as *example* in verse 12 literally means "to strike with force, leaving an impression or mark." It's like the old-fashioned typewriters where the key would strike the paper through a ribbon with ink on it, leaving an inked impression of a particular letter or symbol. We all leave an impression or mark on people. We are typing on the souls of those around us, leaving messages of who we are and what we value and believe, even when we are not consciously doing so.

Sometime back, I caught a portion of a radio program where the speaker referred to studies that showed that even the most introverted people influence a minimum of one thousand people in their lifetime. If that is accurate, then the "example factor" in most people's lives is far greater than many have realized. Each of the thousand people who have been influenced will, in turn, influence one thousand more, the ripple going out further and further!

And the astonishing thing about such figures is that most people aren't introverted!

Areas to Consider

In his encouragement to Timothy to be an example, Paul lists some important areas to consider:

- *In word.* Words carry power—for good or for bad, for life or for death. Some struggle daily with both emotional and self-esteem issues due to unkind and hurtful words spoken to them by some authority figure somewhere in their life. Proverbs 18:21 states, *"Death and life are in the power of the tongue."* Be careful what you say (especially as a habit of life), for words are like seeds that fall into the soil of your and other people's lives, eventually bringing a harvest.

- *Conduct.* This refers to the totality of your life—in church, out of church, at home, at work, at play. The key here is to live a consistent life. Don't be one person in church and someone else outside of it. Live a well-balanced life where your job is not your god (even though you have diligent work habits). Enjoy hobbies, love your family, and be faithful to the Lord and His house.

- *Love.* Be quick to forgive those who have wronged you. Be generous. Be like your heavenly Father.

- *Spirit.* Carry with you an attitude of genuine gratitude and humility.

- *Faith.* Others are inspired to trust God and rely upon His promises when they see the confidence you display in Him—especially in the hard times.

- *Purity.* Your lifestyle will serve to either encourage holiness, or embolden people to sin. What you do and how you live does matter.

- *Doctrine.* Make sure that what you teach and pass on is thoroughly scriptural.

- *Gifting.* Don't let the gifts God has placed in your life remain dormant. *Discover* them, *develop* them, and *dedicate them to God.*

This is, of course, only a partial list. My purpose here is not to give a lengthy exposition of each of these areas, but to simply make you aware that *every* young person is an example and is leaving an imprint upon someone's life.

TRAIL MARKERS FOR THE OLDER GENERATION

Trail Marker #1: Embrace the Fact That God Is Using Young People to Accomplish His Plans (It's Nothing New!)

Young people have always played a significant role in God's plans. David was only a teenager when God called him and began using him. Jeremiah was only a youth when God gave him a word for the nation. Timothy was young when Paul entrusted him with much responsibility and authority. In the story of Job, it was Elihu, the young man, who spoke for God after Job's older friends failed to bring wisdom to his terrible situation.

Several of the key ministries in our church are either run by or have been developed by young men and women.

Our community evangelism and outreach ministries were (for the most part) developed and launched by a young man in his twenties who was saved in our church. For many years our Sunday evening services were led by young men in their twenties.

We have young people involved in virtually every aspect of church life, from missions, to finance, to preaching, to praying, to planning.

We must not give in to the temptation to discount or tune out young people just because they are young. They can and will be used by God, and they do have a perspective we need.

Trail Marker #2: Realize That God Still Looks at the Heart

It has been my observation over the last thirty-five years that many times God uses the most unlikely vessels to do great things. He seems to delight in raising up underdogs and choosing those whom people have overlooked.

When Samuel was given the task by God to anoint Israel's next king from among Jesse's sons, he was sure that Eliab had to be God's choice. Eliab was tall, handsome, and strong... he looked like "kingly material." But consider what God said to Samuel as Eliab stood before him,

> *But the LORD said to Samuel, "Do not look at his appearance or at his physical stature, because I have refused him. For the LORD does not see as man sees; for man looks at the outward appearance, but the LORD looks at the heart." (1 Samuel 16:7)*

Don't Waste Your Time

Shortly after I was saved, there was an older person in my church who actually showed some interest in me. It was very significant for me because many of the people in church seemed to avoid me and treat me like an outsider. Looking back, I'm sure it was because I looked so different than them (I had long hair, a long beard, and I dressed in a very dissimilar fashion from them), and they were actually a little afraid of me. But it was refreshing to my soul to have even one person take some time with me.

Then one of the key leaders in the church took that person aside and told them (referring to me), "Don't waste your time on that guy. He will never amount to anything. If you want to do something worthwhile, spend time with that friend of his that he brought to church… now *he* has potential!"

My friend that I brought to church (whom the leader said had potential) still hasn't become a Christian. I have prayed for him for thirty-five years, and I believe that one day he will come to know the Savior.

Perhaps if you would have seen me back then, you might have felt the same about me as that Christian leader did. I'm glad God saw something in me that others didn't.

Dancing in the Woods

When I was in Bible school, I met a couple who had come out of a very similar background as mine. We immediately became friends. One day as we were having lunch in my apartment, we began talking about our pasts and, not too surprisingly, we had shared an affinity for the same kinds of illegal drugs. They proceeded to tell me how after they would take one particular drug, they would spend time dancing in the woods… naked.

YOUNG PEOPLE HAVE ALWAYS PLAYED A SIGNIFICANT ROLE IN GOD'S PLANS.

After we graduated, they spent some time in a particular Central American country. God used them in an amazing way. They had an enormous impact on the presidential family, teaching a Bible study and ministering to the president's wife to be filled with the Holy Spirit. They also ministered to some of the top military leaders while they were there. Yes, the "woodland fairy dancers" were chosen and sent by God to influence a nation!

The Scripture declares it clearly:

> *26 For you see your calling, brethren, that not many wise according to the flesh, not many mighty, not many noble, are called. 27 But God has chosen the foolish things of the world to put to shame the wise, and God has chosen the weak things of the world to put to shame the things which are mighty; 28 and the base things of the world and the things which are despised God has chosen, and the things which are not, to bring to nothing the things that are, 29 that no flesh should glory in His presence.* (1 Corinthians 1:26-29)

May we earnestly endeavor not to judge the younger generation by outward appearance and thereby underestimate what God plans to do through them. The Lord still looks at the heart.

Trail Marker #3: Lead by Example, Not by Dictate

In 1 Peter 5:1-3 we are told,

> *1 The elders who are among you I exhort, I who am a fellow elder and a witness of the sufferings of Christ, and also a partaker of the glory that will be revealed: 2 Shepherd the flock of God which is among you, serving as overseers, not by compulsion but willingly, not for dishonest gain but eagerly; 3 nor as being lords over those entrusted to you, but being examples to the flock.*

Verse 3 from The Living Bible reads: "*Don't be tyrants, but lead them by your good example.*" The Amplified version reads: "*Not domineering [as arrogant, dictatorial, and overbearing persons] over those in your charge, but being examples (patterns and models of Christian living)…*"

We must guard against becoming dictatorial in our leadership. Wherever you find the type of leadership that dominates those under them, there will eventually be one of two results: (1) crushed creativity and depressed spirits; or (2) rebellion.

The goal of a spiritual father is to bring his children to a place of maturity and freedom where they can express who they are and the ideas God has given them (hopefully enhanced by the example and wisdom imparted from the father). We want to reach, raise, and *release* the younger generation.

Trail Marker #4: Rejoice in the Success of Those Who Come After You

We must guard our hearts against jealousy when our spiritual children go beyond us in their achievements.

In the book of Genesis, Jacob rebuked his son Joseph for his dream and said, *"Shall your mother and I and your brothers indeed come and bow to the earth before you?"* (Genesis 37:10). At first, he recoiled at the thought of his son becoming greater than him; but wisely, he didn't utterly reject it—the Bible says he *"kept the matter in mind"* (Genesis 37:11).

Don't be one of the older generation who supports and applauds someone in the younger generation until they begin to do well. Instead, be one who rejoices in the success of those younger than you.

As Big as Ours

Many years ago, I was in a church service where the senior pastor began to promote the young assistant pastor before the congregation. "He's a fine young man and very gifted. One day he may build a church of his own that's as big as ours—maybe even bigger!" the senior pastor declared.

Well, that young man did go on to build a bigger church—fifty times bigger, in fact—in just a few years. Unfortunately, the senior pastor who'd been his biggest cheerleader then severed their relationship. He felt threatened. And when it came right down to it, he didn't like the notoriety and attention the young man and his church were getting.

A Reflection on You

When you have sown good things into a person's life and they begin to prosper and multiply, it should be cause for rejoicing. In reality, their success is a reflection on you. It means you have done your job well.

The dream of some professional athletes is to become a coach once they retire from their sport. And for some, the ultimate blessing would be to coach for the same club or team they played for themselves.

Imagine if that retired player-turned-coach leads his team to the championship. He is not going to be upset or jealous because the team he coached beat the record of the team he played with. He is going to be ecstatic! The new team's success is a reflection of his excellent coaching. They excelled because he excelled as a coach.

Golf, Anyone?

My oldest son, Harrison, began golfing when he was fifteen. I taught him everything I knew about the game. For about a year and a half, I could thrash him soundly. Then things began to change. Sometime before he turned seventeen, he ran away from me. He began to play for his school team, and his game lifted to a level where I could no longer compete with him. I didn't get mad when he started driving the ball forty yards past me. I didn't withdraw and refuse to play with him when he became deadly with his short irons. Whenever he hit another amazing shot, I would just brag to the other people in our group, "That's my son!"

May we learn to humbly rejoice and thank God as the younger generation goes beyond where we have been and begins to do more than we have ever done. After all, their success is a statement that we have done our job well!

In the next chapter, we will find a blueprint from one of the greatest Christian leaders of all time on how to work successfully with the younger generation.

TAKE ACTION

CHAPTER THREE

Meditation

I meditate on all Your works; I muse on the work of Your hands.
(Psalm 143:5)

Points to Ponder

1. The heart that embraces an honoring attitude toward seniors brings blessing from God.

2. You need to let the truth move from your ears to your feet (act upon it) before it will benefit you or anyone else through you.

3. Young people need to realize that their lives are making an impact on others. It is not just the older folks whom people look to as examples.

4. God seems to delight in using unlikely vessels to do great things.

5. We must guard our hearts against jealousy when our spiritual children go beyond us in their achievements.

Our Final Authority—God's Word

Your word is a lamp to my feet and a light to my path. (Psalm 119:105)

Leviticus 19:32 (GNT)

"_____ for _____

and _____ them. Reverently _____ ;

I am the LORD."

Proverbs 13:1

A _____ heeds his father's _____,

but a _____ does not _____ rebuke.

3 John 1:4

I have no _____ than to hear

that _____ walk _____ .

1 Timothy 4:12

Let no one despise _____ *, but be*

an _____ *to the believers in*

_____ *, in* _____ *,*

in _____ *, in* _____ *,*

in _____ *, in* _____ *.*

1 Samuel 16:7

But the LORD said to Samuel, "Do not look at his

_____ *or at his* _____

_____ *, because I have refused him. For the*

LORD does not _____ *;*

for man looks at the _____ *,*

but the LORD looks at the _____ *."*

Application

What portions of the chapter stood out to you? Why? In what ways might they apply to you?

In what ways could you act upon and implement some of the principles brought out in this chapter? (Write down your thoughts and ideas. Even if they are rough and incomplete at this point, they will help you gain clarity and focus, and hopefully move you toward action.)

_____

_____

_____

_____

_____

_____

_____

_____

_____

_____

_____

_____

_____

_____

Group Discussion

Without counsel, plans go awry, but in the multitude of counselors they are established. (Proverbs 15:22)

Share your thoughts and insights about the chapter. Don't hesitate to ask questions. Many times you will find that others were wondering about the same things.

Questions to Get You Started

Q. What points in the chapter do you strongly agree with? Why?

Q. Were there any points that you disagreed with? Why?

Q. How would you describe an honoring attitude?

Q. Do you think many young people realize their lives are serving as examples to others?

Q. Why does God tend to use unlikely vessels to accomplish His work?

Q. What do you feel the Holy Spirit is saying to you about what you have studied so far?

Game Plan

Deal bountifully with Your servant, that I may live; and I will observe Your word [hearing, receiving, loving, and obeying it]. (Psalm 119:17 AMP)

Steps I will personally take to help connect the generations:

1. _____

2. _____

3. _____

Prayer

"Therefore I say to you, whatever things you ask when you pray, believe that you receive them, and you will have them." (Mark 11:24)

Talk to God about what you have discovered and discussed.

If you have not had an honoring attitude toward those of an older generation, repent and ask for God's help as you endeavor to adopt an attitude of heart that is pleasing to Him.

If you have overlooked or disregarded those of a younger generation, repent and ask for God's help to both recognize and encourage the potential in the younger members of the church.

Earnestly pray for a multigenerational church and seek to know your part in supporting it and bringing it about.

A BLUEPRINT

The apostle Paul was a man who thought, planned, and acted generationally. Though he brought many to Christ, there are only three men in Scripture whom he specifically calls his *sons*. They are Timothy, Titus, and Onesimus.

There are six outstanding elements about his relationships with them that we can learn from and apply to what we are discovering about the generations.

1. He Delivered Them

When a woman gives birth to a baby, we say she *delivered* a child. Paul was personally involved in the *new birth* experience of all three of these young men. He brought them to Christ.

Timothy was most likely converted during Paul's first missionary journey as he preached the Gospel in the cities of Lystra and Derbe. Upon returning to those same cities to confirm the churches during his second missionary journey, Paul was accompanied by Timothy, who had a good reputation among the brethren there (Acts 16:1-3).

We are not told exactly how or when Titus came to the Lord, only that Paul refers to him as "*a true son in our common faith*" (Titus 1:4).

Onesimus was won to Christ while Paul was a prisoner in Rome and then sent back to Philemon with the letter bearing Philemon's name (Philemon 1:8-21).

Whether he was visiting a local synagogue, addressing Greek philosophers on the Areopagus, or sitting chained in a Roman prison cell, Paul was always engaged in the business of winning souls. He made the most of every opportunity, and some of his "sons" were brought to faith in Christ under some of the most adverse conditions.

In whatever circumstances you find yourself today, however difficult things may seem, God can still use you—if you will make yourself available. Don't wait for perfect conditions before you sow your seed. Plant the Gospel in someone's heart today. You may be surprised at the result. Some of God's greatest treasures are found during difficult times and in unusual places.

Keep on Sharing

To those a little further down the track in their relationship with the Lord, I want to encourage you to continue sharing your faith in Christ with those who don't know Him yet.

What typically happens to people when they come to a genuine faith in Christ is that the world of their family and personal relationships is shaken. Everyone can see the change that has taken place in a person's life, and lots of questions are asked. Some are quite happy with what has happened, while others may not be. However, regardless of how individuals respond, the good news is Jesus is being talked about and people are being either directly or indirectly confronted with the Gospel message.

Generally, some of those who have heard and seen the impact that Christ has made in the life of their family member or friend will come to faith and be saved as well. It's certainly not unusual during the first year after a person is converted—almost without trying—for a number of family, friends, and acquaintances to be swept into the Kingdom soon after.

Yet, after that initial "shaking up" with family and friends, many Christians no longer see others coming to Christ. In fact, some Christians have not been directly involved in the conversion of a lost soul for many years. Often, after a person has been a Christian for a while, they are absorbed into the life of the church and spend very little time with any unsaved people, if at all. Their life and most of their time revolves around Christian friends and Christian events—they live in a kind of Christian bubble.

We need to consciously burst that bubble and forge some relationships with people who don't know the Lord, in order to create opportunities to bring them to the Lord.

2. He Deposited into Them

Paul endeavored to spend time with these young men. And through association, personal teaching, prayer, personal ministry… as well as communicating with them via the letters that bear their names… he made rich spiritual deposits in their lives. His words to his son in the faith, Timothy, exhibit this well in 2 Timothy 1:3, 6.

> ^{3} *I thank God, whom I serve with a pure conscience, as my forefathers did, as without ceasing I remember you in my prayers night and day…. * ^{6} *Therefore I remind you to stir up the gift of God which is in you through the laying on of my hands.*

Paul prayed consistently for Timothy and imparted into his life through the laying on of hands. God may or may not impart a spiritual gift when you lay hands on someone, but there is a blessing in your hands that can be transmitted if you will put them on the appropriate people and declare it.

The patriarchs of old would gather their children, lay hands on them, and declare blessings over them that impacted their futures. Both your natural and spiritual children need your blessing. (You might want to take a moment right now to look at your hands and say out loud, "There is a blessing in my hands.") Speak a blessing over those you love and for whom you pray. Put your hands on them and ask God to guide, help, and strengthen them.

GOD CAN STILL USE YOU—IF YOU WILL MAKE YOURSELF AVAILABLE.

As our children were growing up, we would ask any minister of stature who spoke in our church (someone with a long record of faithfulness, good character, and fruitfulness) to lay hands on our kids and bless them. Over the years, they have had some amazing and sometimes unusual blessings spoken over their lives. And though Janet and I considered this to be important for our kids, we realized that by far the most important hands that would ever be laid on them and the most significant blessings that would ever be spoken over them were our own.

In the same way, I believe it is important for spiritual parents to deposit into the lives of those they help win to Christ. In this age of hyper-technology and long-distance instant communication, it is even more important to take the time to talk with, listen to, and personally interact with those God has given us the privilege of mentoring.

3. He Duplicated Himself in Them

Paul duplicated himself in his spiritual sons. This was partly accomplished through his teaching and instruction, but as it is with natural fathers and their sons, *a lot more is caught than taught.*

As these three men associated with Paul, his lifestyle, values, and attitudes were transmitted to them. His life became a blueprint for them to follow.

Paul reveals this in his second letter to Timothy. In 2 Timothy 3:10-11, Paul says to Timothy,

> [10] *But you have carefully followed my doctrine, manner of life, purpose, faith, longsuffering, love, perseverance,* [11] *persecutions, afflictions, which happened to me at Antioch, at Iconium, at Lystra—what persecutions I endured. And out of them all the Lord delivered me.*

The phrase *carefully followed* could literally be translated "traced out a pattern." His life had literally become a blueprint or pattern that his sons could imitate. They observed his trust in God during the hard times, they saw his attitude when he had been wronged, they watched his steadfastness and tenacity as he continued to move ever forward in the purposes of God. And they witnessed the faithfulness of the Lord as He intervened time and again in Paul's life. In Paul, they had an example to follow.

When Paul wrote to the Corinthians about Titus being among them, he asked, *"Did we not walk in the same spirit? Did we not walk in the same steps?"* (2 Corinthians 12:18). Paul knew the answer before he asked the question because he had duplicated himself in Titus.

My wife and I were attending a minister's conference in California many years ago. The conference was being led by a well-known statesman/pastor in his home church. One of the afternoon sessions was being taught by one of the pastors on his team. I was listening intently when I suddenly realized how much he sounded like the senior pastor.

His choice of words, his inflections, his very spirit seemed to emulate the man he had trained under. As I continued to watch and listen, I noticed that even his mannerisms and way of moving about the platform were similar to his mentor.

It's not that his own personality had been swallowed up or that he was being untrue to whom God had created him to be as a person—that was all intact and being expressed as well. What I observed actually encouraged my heart. The positive aspects of leadership, humility, and eloquence in communication had been successfully transmitted, just as it had been done with Paul and his sons in the Lord.

If those of us who are leaders would realize how we are daily creating patterns for others to follow, perhaps we might be a little more purposeful in the examples we set. Paul's duplication into the lives of Timothy, Titus, and Onesimus was something he did consciously and deliberately.

4. He Delegated to Them

Paul raised up sons and then *released* them. First and Second Timothy are filled with instructions for Timothy to oversee the churches with which he had been entrusted and for which he was responsible. Titus was sent on an important mission to the church in Corinth, and Paul delegated to him the oversight of the churches in Crete—a job that wasn't for the faint of heart.

As we read about Crete and the difficulty of Titus's mission there, we begin to get an idea of how much Paul trusted him.

> [4] *To Titus, a true son in our common faith: Grace, mercy, and peace from God the Father and the Lord Jesus Christ our Savior.* [5] *For this reason I left you in Crete, that you should set in order the things that*

are lacking, and appoint elders in every city as I commanded you...

[12] One of them, a prophet of their own, said, "Cretans are always liars, evil beasts, lazy gluttons." [13] This testimony is true. Therefore rebuke them sharply, that they may be sound in the faith. (Titus 1:4-5, 12-13)

Who would want to oversee that bunch? Paul knew Titus was equal to the task. He had trained him and poured into him, and now Titus was ready to be released. Why train someone if you never plan on releasing him or her? Why develop someone if you never delegate any responsibility or authority to that person? To be trained and never used is not only a waste of effort and ability, but also disheartening to the one who has been prepared.

Although Paul would have personally benefitted from the ministry of Onesimus in Rome, he released him to be reconciled to Philemon in Colossae and to serve the church that met in his home.

According to Colossians 4:7-9, Onesimus was also sent, along with Tychicus, to comfort the believers at Colossae and bring them news concerning Paul. It is very likely that Onesimus carried the Colossian letter to the church there, as well as carrying the New Testament letter to Philemon.

Paul gave all of these young men both responsibility and authority. He entrusted important tasks to them that would have eternal consequences. He delegated to them, knowing it was an important aspect of leadership and a vital ingredient in church growth.

Don't Snatch the Pole

One day I had the chance to watch a father teach his son to fish. You could tell the boy was happy to be there, and that dad should be commended for taking the time to be with his son. But his method of teaching left a lot to be desired.

Every time the boy got a bite, the father would snatch the pole out of his hands, set the hook, and reel in the fish while his son stood by and watched. I don't know if that father was afraid his son would lose the fish or what, but the boy never got to even try to fight and land a fish on his own.

A LOT MORE IS CAUGHT THAN TAUGHT.

This reminds me of how some Christian leaders do ministry. They instruct on what and how they want things done, but in the end they always snatch the pole away from their spiritual sons and do the work themselves.

I believe it's better to truly delegate—even if a few fish are lost due to inexperience. In the end much more will be accomplished, and there will be some seasoned fishermen we can rely on to get the job done.

5. He Delighted in Them

Paul never looked at his spiritual sons as just resources or tools to be used. They were *family*, and he was devoted to them.

In the book of Philemon, Paul referred to Onesimus as *"my own heart"* (Philemon 1:12). You can't read Paul's letters to Timothy without feeling the deep bond that existed between them. And when Paul came to Troas to preach, even though a door was opened to him by the Lord, he had no rest in his spirit because he didn't find Titus (2 Corinthians 2:12-13)!

Paul carried them in his heart and they were dear to him. He delighted in and was completely devoted to them. He never thought of them as replaceable or exploitable resources.

More Than a Monthly Check

Many years ago, a friend of mine supported a man's organization with a substantial monthly sum of money. The man he supported was a bit of a legend in Christian circles, and looked up to by many for his wisdom and unconventional leadership. Some of the projects he was engaged in and leading were enormous in both scope and impact.

My friend treasured the relationship he had with this man. He was one of the "favored sons" and was given much attention... until he experienced a personal financial downturn. Due to a situation that arose, he had to scale back on his support of this ministry temporarily. Immediately, he was discarded and given no more time with or access to the man he'd considered his mentor.

Sadly, he realized he had been looked upon all along as just a resource to be used. He was only valuable to this man as long as he could write a monthly check to the organization.

A true father in the faith never looks at those he is raising up as merely a means to achieving a goal. Those who are committed to the next generation genuinely love those they have been called to work with and train up.

If you are a young person who is reading this right now, listen carefully to me. If I could sit down with you wherever you are right now, I would look into your eyes and tell you, *"You are valuable and you are loved. God loves you more than you could ever possibly understand, and there are people who, while appreciating whatever gifts you bring to the table, love you and value you as a person regardless of whether or not you contribute."*

And for those of you who are of the older generation reading this, invest in the next generation regardless of personal gain. Your job… our job… is to faithfully love, support, and trust the younger men and women whom God has called us to work with.

William

Shortly after I was saved, I shared Christ with an old friend. I'll call him "William." In the old days, we used to drink and take drugs together. He showed no interest in the Gospel when I initially talked to him. But I was burdened for his soul, so I continued to speak to him about Jesus whenever I had the opportunity. I also prayed for him regularly.

During that time, the local college was planning to host a free concert by a Christian band, so I invited William. He thanked me for the invitation but indicated he had better things to do. So I went to the concert, which ended up being attended by about 200 people. After about an hour and a half of music, one of the band members invited the audience to accept Christ. The whole place grew silent as one lone figure from the back of the auditorium rose to his feet and began making his way forward.

He was sobbing so violently that he looked as though he might collapse. When he finally reached the front, a Christian worker embraced him. He continued to cry for several more minutes, and eventually he prayed and received Christ as his Savior that night. I was filled with an indescribable sense of awe mingled with joy at the sight of it, because the one person who responded to the invitation that night was my friend William.

Mentoring a New Convert

Although I hadn't been saved for very long myself, I began teaching William everything I knew about the Lord. We spent many hours studying the Bible together. I even had the privilege of laying hands on him to receive the Holy Spirit. In many ways, I looked at our new spiritual relationship as a father-son situation. I didn't know much, but I imparted what I knew. And I continued to pray for him.

All was well for a season until a girl from William's past suddenly appeared on the scene. The more time he spent with her, the more his relationship with Jesus deteriorated. I watched some of his old sinful patterns begin to creep back into his life, and eventually it came to the point where he decided that it would best if we parted ways.

TO BE TRAINED AND NEVER USED IS DISHEARTENING.

When William began to fall away from his relationship with the Lord, it broke my heart. I was tied to him. I played an instrumental part in bringing him to Christ. I had poured my life into him, and it had been the delight of my heart to watch him grow in the Lord. It wasn't something I could just disengage myself from.

Close to four decades have come and gone since my ministry to William, and I still think of him fairly often. I still pray for him. I don't know where he is or what his life is like, but I can't forget about my "son in the Lord."

Mothers and fathers in Christ are devoted to and delight in their children. They *have no greater joy than to hear that their children walk in truth* (see 3 John 1:4). At the same time, however, there is no greater sorrow than to know that one of your spiritual children has strayed from the path.

Regardless, our job is to be faithful.

6. He Depended upon Them

Paul sent his spiritual sons on important missions that involved delivering his letters, overseeing the churches, and handling large sums of money; but by far the most important thing he expected of them was to become spiritual fathers themselves. He had passed the baton to them, and now he depended on them to pass it to those coming after them. Consider these words of encouragement to Timothy,

> *¹ You therefore, my son, be strong in the grace that is in Christ Jesus. ² And the things that you have heard from me among many witnesses, commit these to faithful men who will be able to teach others also.* (2 Timothy 2:1-2)

In writing to his son Titus, Paul admonishes him to be a pattern for others to follow in all areas of life (Titus 2:7-8).

If the children don't reproduce, the work dies and the mission ceases with them.

Among the greatest gifts you can give to a father are grandchildren. For so long, Janet and I have listened to joyful grandparents go on and on about their grandkids. We always thought most of them were way too excited and wondered, *What's the big deal?* That is, until we had grandkids of our own! It's almost weird how much you can love them, taking joy in the littlest things they do.

Proverbs 17:6 (NLT) says, *"Grandchildren are the crowning glory of the aged."* When your spiritual children begin winning others to Christ and pouring their lives into them, it is a crown of glory to you. A sense of godly pride is associated with that. When one of your sons or daughters introduces their spiritual children to you, you know you've had some measure of success in your role as a mentor.

It's an old saying, but it is still brimming with truth: *"Success isn't success without a successor."*

Our job as a spiritual father or mother is not finished until we produce spiritual offspring who are reproducing themselves in others.

In our church, we are doing our best to reach, raise up, and release young people. Part of what we are telling them and endeavoring to put into them is that they *must* continue to do the same thing. The future depends on it, and we are depending on them.

Our Supreme Example

Jesus is our supreme example of a spiritual mentor. He spent three years training up His disciples in order to release them with the message of redemption for the world.

In John 17:4, in His High Priestly prayer, Jesus says to the Father, *"I have glorified You on the earth. I have finished the work which You have given Me to do."* These are the words Jesus spoke to the Father just prior to His arrest and crucifixion. How could He have finished the work that the Father had given Him to do? He hadn't gone to the cross yet. He hadn't paid for mankind's sins yet. That was accomplished in John 19:30 when Jesus said, *"It is finished,"* just as He died.

The work Jesus spoke of finishing in John 17:4 had to do with training His disciples so they could carry the message of redemption. That is made clear by the next statements He made in John 17:6-8, 18 and 20.

OUR JOB IS NOT FINISHED UNTIL WE PRODUCE SPIRITUAL OFFSPRING WHO ARE REPRODUCING THEMSELVES IN OTHERS.

> [6] *"I have manifested Your name to the men whom You have given Me out of the world. They were Yours, You gave them to Me, and they have kept Your word.* [7] *Now they have known that all things which You have given Me are from You.* [8] *For I have given to them the words which You have given Me; and they have received them, and have known surely that I came forth from You; and they have believed that You sent Me....* [18] *As You sent Me into the world, I also have sent them into the world....* [20] *I do not pray for these alone, but also for those who will believe in Me through their word."*

Jesus had to finish the work of training and developing His disciples before He went to the cross. If He hadn't, the message of God's love and salvation wouldn't have been carried and transmitted to the coming generations.

Directly or indirectly, every believer in every generation has come to know Christ through the ministry of these men (through what they preached, taught, and wrote). But that never would have occurred if Jesus hadn't been committed to reaching, raising up, and releasing others.

Let's follow His example and the example of the apostle Paul by *delivering, depositing, duplicating, delegating, delighting,* and *depending.*

CHAPTER FOUR

Meditation

"This Book of the Law shall not depart from your mouth, but you shall meditate in it day and night, that you may observe to do according to all that is written in it. For then you will make your way prosperous, and then you will have good success." (Joshua 1:8)

Points to Ponder

1. Part of being a "father in the faith" involves winning people to Christ.

2. Many believers have little or no contact with people outside of their church. However, if we are going to plant the seeds of the Gospel and win people to the Lord, we must forge relationships with those who do not yet know Him.

3. As leaders, we are daily creating patterns for others to follow.

Those whom we mentor will consciously and unconsciously catch and emulate our example.

4. We are to raise up and train others in order to release them. If we never truly delegate authority and responsibility, we haven't done our job.

5. People are not just resources or tools to be used. We need to be genuinely devoted to those under our leadership.

6. Jesus spent over three years training and developing the disciples so they might carry the Good News of God's love to the world.

Our Final Authority—God's Word

Your word I have hidden in my heart, that I might not sin against You. (Psalm 119:11)

2 Timothy 1:6

Therefore I remind you to _____ the _____

which is in you through the _____ of my hands.

2 Timothy 3:10-11

[10] *But you have _____*

my doctrine, manner of life, _____ , faith,

_____ , love, _____ ,

¹¹ persecutions, _____ , which happened to me at Antioch, at Iconium, at Lystra—what persecutions I endured. And out of them all the Lord _____ .

2 Timothy 2:1-2

¹ You therefore, my son, be strong _____ that is in Christ Jesus. ² And the things that you have _____ _____ among many witnesses, _____ these to _____ men who will be able to _____ also.

John 17:4

"I have glorified _____ . I have _____ the work which You have _____ ."

John 17:20

"I do not _____ for these alone, but also for those who will _____ their word."

Application

What portions of the chapter stood out to you? Why? In what ways might they apply to you?

In what ways could you act upon and implement some of the principles brought out in this chapter? (Write down your thoughts and ideas. Even if they are rough and incomplete at this point, they will help you gain clarity and focus, and hopefully move you toward action.)

Group Discussion

Better a poor and wise youth than an old and foolish king who will be admonished no more. (Ecclesiastes 4:13)

Begin the discussion by asking what thoughts or statements in the chapter stood out to or arrested the attention of those present.

Questions to Get You Started

Q. When you first came to Christ, did others among your family or friends also come to faith shortly thereafter?

Q. Do you still have people in your personal world that you can share the Gospel with, or are you in a "Christian bubble"?

Q. Did you ever consider that God has put a blessing in your hands that you might impart to someone else?

Q. Have you ever experienced the frustration (or perhaps been the cause) of being trained but never trusted (released with responsibility and authority)?

Q. How did it make you feel? Why? What could have been done (on both sides) to resolve the issue?

Q. Have you ever been tempted to look at someone merely as a resource to be used and not as a unique person to be valued?

Q. How can we guard our hearts against this happening?

Q. Is there anyone in your life that you are pouring into at this time?

Game Plan

"Whatever He says to you, do it." (John 2:5)

Steps I will personally take to help connect the generations:

1. _____

2. _____

3. _____

Prayer

"Call to me, and I will answer you, and show you great and mighty things, which you do not know." (Jeremiah 33:3)

Time to talk to God and time to listen. Remember, prayer is a two-way street. Make your requests known, but also take time to be quiet and listen for His answers.

If you have ever been trained but not trusted, perhaps a prayer of forgiveness may be in order, along with an earnest request for God to help and bless the person(s) who failed to release you to do what you'd been trained to do.

If you were the leader who failed to trust and release those whom you trained, it might be in order for you to ask for God's help.

Perhaps a past betrayal has made it hard to trust and release others, or maybe you never had a proper model to follow. Whatever the cause, God is ready to help those who call upon Him.

Pray for God's wisdom and guidance as you move forward in reaching, raising up, and releasing others.

CHAPTER FIVE

BUYING IN

I have done my best to make my case for both embracing and working to have a multigenerational church. A church where at least three generations are all experiencing the empowerment of the Holy Spirit *together*, serving and leading *together*, and reaping a mighty harvest of lost souls *together*.

Now I'd like to ask and answer some questions—first to those who consider themselves to be a part of the older generation, then to our younger coworkers.

QUESTIONS FOR THE OLDER GENERATION

1. Why should you buy in?

   a. <u>Because it is God's idea</u>. His plan to work simultaneously with multiple generations is written across the recorded history of Scripture. Not only is it His idea, but it is His invitation for us to join Him in the endeavor.

   Prayer is not just about God answering us; it is about us answering God. I, for one, am saying *yes* to God's call. You have read more than my heart in this book. I believe it is God's heart as well.

   One day we will stand before Him to give an account for our lives. May we be able to say with confidence, "I responded to Your call to connect the generations; I helped pass the baton."

b. <u>Because we must succeed in this in order to effectively reach the world for Christ</u>. The gifts, resources, influence, and creative insight required to reach this amazingly diverse and alarmingly lost world do not just reside in one generation. God, in His wisdom, spread out what is needed across at least three generations.

c. <u>Because our youth are valuable</u>. Let us not forget that a few short years ago, *we were them*. Our young people are worth the investment of our time, resources, and effort.

d. <u>Because if we don't reach and engage the younger generation in Kingdom work, in all likelihood, we will lose them</u>. The world is not sitting idly by when it comes to reaching the younger generations. Vast sums of money and research are being invested to capture the hearts of our youth.

PRAYER IS NOT JUST ABOUT GOD ANSWERING US; IT IS ABOUT US ANSWERING GOD.

The reality is only the Church holds the key to satisfy the hunger of the younger generations. They are looking for something bigger than themselves to be a part of, something radical and transformational. Something that can bring practical help and lasting change to the global problems we are facing.

What better way to direct them than to the cause of Christ? They will give their hearts to **something**. Many of them are willing to sacrifice for an ideal. The world is selling lots of cheap imitations. If we never present them with the genuine article and challenge them with the adventure of following Jesus, what are they to do?

Let us determine that we will enlist them in this great end-times drama of rescuing the perishing, lifting the downtrodden, and transforming society in Jesus' name!

2. What will it cost you?

a. Time

b. Effort

c. Money (almost all Kingdom endeavors have a material cost)

d. The occasional unpleasantness but necessity of change (the moment we stop changing, we start dying)

3. What will it mean to you in practical terms?

a. Opening up your life and seizing opportunities to speak up and share

As the psalmist says in Psalm 79:13 (NIV),

> *Then we your people, the sheep of your pasture,*
> *will praise you forever; from generation to*
> *generation we will recount your praise*

Then there is this powerful word found in Psalm 89:1 (NASB),

> *I will sing of the lovingkindness of the LORD*
> *forever; To all generations I will make known*
> *Thy faithfulness with my mouth.*

Notice the words *we will* and *I will* from these verses. "We," as members of local churches, must embrace what God is doing; and "I," as an individual, must determine to get involved in the process. This is not something that can be done from a distance. It will require up-close, personal attention. It will affect you personally; and once you say *yes*, God will give you opportunities to invest into a young person's life.

I Know How to Barbecue

There is no need to make this more complex than it needs to be. I realize there are those who will want to dissect this into the tiniest parts possible, and then come up with charts and long lists of how to properly mentor young people. Don't let those types of people scare you away. I personally take a much easier approach. I don't get the charts and detailed lists, but I do know how to barbecue.

THERE ARE NECESSARY SACRIFICES AND UNNECESSARY SACRIFICES.

On occasion, Janet and I invite a bunch of young people over, and I barbecue for them. We hang out and eat, laugh, and tell stories. We might have a short time of prayer, and I answer any questions they might have. It's all very low-key and extremely informal.

We just hang out.

Recently, Janet has been inviting a group of young women to the house to watch relationship videos. They eat and talk and talk and talk… and I make myself scarce. But it has been a great way to engage, help, and encourage those from a younger generation. Do what fits you and your personality, but don't overthink it. Just invite someone younger than you into your world.

b. Being conscious that your example speaks louder than your words

In Philippians 3:17, Paul tells us,

Brethren, join in following my example, and note those who so walk, as you have us for a pattern.

Many years back, when our oldest son was quite young, he and I were in the car together. I rolled the window down and spit out the open window. My son intently watched me from his child's car seat, and then he turned and spit as well—only his window wasn't rolled down! He then looked back at me with a huge grin that seemed to say, "Isn't it great, Dad? I'm just like you!"

In a similar way, young believers are more impacted by our example than most people realize. We are being observed all the time. The expression of our faith in God when we are faced with difficulties, our lifestyles, priorities, integrity, marriages, and worshiping hearts are all continually on display, even when we aren't aware of it. Our lives are serving as examples and patterns for others to follow.

As Your Fathers Did, So Do You

The Scripture makes some startling statements when it comes to the power of a negative example. Just before Stephen was stoned, he said to his persecutors concerning their resisting the Holy Spirit, *"As your fathers did, so do you"* (Acts 7:51). God said of His own people in Ezekiel 20:24, *"Their eyes were fixed on their fathers' idols."*

As we know, biblically speaking, an idol can be anything that takes the place of or comes before God in a person's life. It could be a sport, a job, a boyfriend or a girlfriend, money—anything that has crept into the number one spot in our hearts, where God alone belongs.

As a preacher, I've had the opportunity to observe a lot of people in ministry over the years. And I've witnessed all too often where the pulpit becomes an idol, crowding out the minister's family, friends, and even their personal time and relationship with God.

It is an inescapable fact that there is a significant sacrifice required in the lives of those who preach the Gospel. My family and I know this firsthand. God calls upon His servants to make sacrifices for the sake of His Kingdom. I call those *necessary sacrifices,* and there is always grace from God to cover and sustain you and your family as you yield to God's plan and make the sacrifices He is calling you to make.

But then there are also *unnecessary sacrifices.* These are sacrifices that are ego-driven. They don't originate from a place of trust in God. They are not Spirit-directed and, in the long run, they always produce grief—especially in the minister's family.

Some call it the "sprinkler syndrome," where the sprinkler spends all its energy watering the grass that is farthest away from it, while neglecting the grass right next to it and closest to it. When the pulpit becomes a "mistress" or an idol, the closer things can begin to dry up and die due to lack of attention—things like marriage, children, even personal friendships, and fellowship with God.

Throughout the years, I've been involved in trying to help many preachers whose marriages and families were disintegrating due to this very thing. On one occasion, I even offered to pay the salaries of a minister and his small staff if he would just take one week off to work on his marriage. (He and his wife were separated, and she was staying with some people from our church.) He refused the offer, preferring to continue with his scheduled meetings. He had time to spend with the people he thought could open doors of opportunity for his ministry, yet he was neglecting his wife. Sadly, their marriage ended in divorce.

Almost without fail, wherever I've seen sad scenarios like this, the mentors of those preachers were exactly the same way. The problem was reproduced because the children's eyes were fixed on their father's idols.

I've used an example from preaching ministry because it is the field I labor in. But I'm quite sure that equally valid examples could be drawn from any field of labor one would care to choose.

Strong Currents

The truth is, there are strong currents emotionally, physically, and spiritually that draw people into following the pattern of their fathers or mentors. When those patterns are negative, it takes a firm and conscious decision to go another way. However, if left to do what comes easily and naturally, we will end up duplicating the patterns that are lived out before us, even when those patterns are destructive.

If you find yourself repeating the negative examples that were modeled for you, make the decision—for your sake and the sake of those who are learning from you—that your life will be one worth following. Even though you won't always do everything perfectly… and you will make your share of mistakes… determine that the overall pattern that your life takes is one worth emulating.

c. Praying about and for the younger generation

David prayed this prayer in Psalm 71:18 (NLT),

> *Now that I am old and gray, do not abandon*
> *me, O God. Let me proclaim your power to*
> *this new generation, your mighty miracles*
> *to all who come after me.*

In essence, David was praying, *God, there are things in me that I have to download to this next generation, but I'm going to need Your strength, wisdom, and sustaining power to get it done.*

He aggressively and specifically prayed concerning his role in helping the next generation. He knew that he'd learned things from God that he had to transmit to those coming after him.

The apostle Paul also prayed for the younger generation as well.

> *My little children, for whom I labor in birth again until*
> *Christ is formed in you.* (Galatians 4:19)

The phrase *I labor in birth* refers to prayer. The first time Paul had labored in birth for them had to do with their salvation. He had preached the Gospel to them and labored in prayer for them.

After the conversion of these people in Galatia, a group had come from Jerusalem, telling them they weren't really saved. They claimed that in order to be saved, one had to accept Christ and keep all the Law of Moses, including circumcision. They caused a huge amount of confusion among these young believers.

So what does Paul do? He writes a letter to them (the book of Galatians) dispelling the error, and he labors in birth *again* for them.

We must realize how important our prayers are for new converts and for young people in general. Once a young person comes to faith in Christ, whether that be through the witness of a friend, a church or youth camp… or any other way God chooses to reach them… they need our prayers!

YOU CAN'T EFFECTIVELY REACH THE WORLD WITHOUT THE WISDOM AND AID OF AN OLDER GENERATION.

Faced with the pull of the world, raging hormones, the evil influences of sin, and the strategies of the devil, our youth need some stable souls who are willing to labor in birth until Christ is formed in them!

On two occasions, I have been told by great men of God that they prayed regularly for me. I was both humbled and stunned. Both of these men were legendary in my mind, having faithfully served God for many years. It encouraged my soul and inspired me to pray for those coming after me. It also made me realize that any success that I achieve can be directly attributed to the prayers of these men (and I'm sure the prayers of many others).

Are you praying regularly for someone in a younger generation? If not, why not start today?

QUESTIONS FOR THE YOUNGER GENERATION

1. Why should you buy in?

a. <u>Because it's God's plan</u>. We have not only the scriptural examples and promises of the different generations working together (which clearly reveal God's heart concerning the issue), but also a blending of voices from around the world, all saying the same thing—this is God's mandate for His Church in this hour. Almost everywhere I go in the world, leaders in the Church are talking about building bridges between the generations.

b. <u>Because you can't effectively reach the world without the wisdom and aid of an older generation</u>. The older folks are the ones with the means and resources to fund the visions and dreams that you, the younger generation, are burning with.

2. What will it cost you?

a. Time

b. Effort

c. The willingness to adapt, listen, and learn

3. What will it mean to you in practical terms?

a. Reaching out and engaging the older generation

You will need to follow the example given in Deuteronomy 32:7,

> *"Remember the days of old, consider the years of many generations. Ask your father, and he will show you; your elders, and they will tell you."*

Ask. As a younger person, engage an older person and ask questions about what he or she has seen and experienced of God. At this stage in your life, some of those in the older generation have learned more by accident than you've learned on purpose.

Consider these admonitions from Job,

"Just ask the former generation. Pay attention to the experience of our ancestors." (Job 8:8 NLT)

"For we're newcomers at this, with a lot to learn, and not too long to learn it." (Job 8:9 The Message)

Goats, Questions, and Prayers

Shortly after I was saved, I met an 80-year-old woman whom everyone called "Mom." She was a wonderful Christian raising six orphans on her own. She also ran a small health food company and preached at different churches around the country. Her life was a sermon about trusting God for strength.

I dropped by on occasion to milk her goats for her, and when I was there, I would always ask her questions. She was always happy to talk to me, and she gave me very good counsel on several occasions.

WE ARE EXPECTING YOU TO EXCEL AND GO BEYOND WHERE WE HAVE BEEN.

But through my times with her, more than anything else, I learned the importance of praying in the Spirit. She always seemed to be praying. She prayed in her car; she prayed while pacing back and forth in her room; and usually, in order to answer one of my questions, she'd have to take a short break from praying!

There were a few other older saints I learned some vital lessons from during those early days in the Lord. One couple named Fred and Eva answered a lot of questions I had about the Holy Spirit. And they laid their hands on me and prayed for me on more than one occasion. To this day, I am grateful for their input.

When Janet and I were young parents, we asked lots of questions of older ministers who had successfully raised their kids. We realized there were unique aspects to being brought up in a minister's home, and we wanted to do the best job we could for our kids. We asked about what they did right and what they did wrong. We wanted to learn as much as possible from other people's mistakes rather than our own.

To this day, I still gravitate to older people, and I still ask lots of questions. I regularly hang out with my dad, and I am still gleaning wisdom from him. (He's full of good old-fashioned common sense.)

Take a Grayhead to Lunch

Young person, listen! Don't make the older people do all the work. Be friendly, be proactive about this, take a grayhead to lunch. Make the effort to engage an older person in conversation, treat them to a meal, and have your questions ready.

Have a heart that honors the older generation, and take their counsel seriously.

b.   Realizing that you still have to fight your own battles

Although those of the older generation can help you if you will listen to them, they can't hand you a conflict-free life on a platter. You will have to learn to fight the good fight of faith, just as we have.

Judges 3:1-2 reminds us of an important principle,

> [1] *Now these are the nations which the LORD left, that He might test Israel by them, that is, all who had not known any of the wars in Canaan*

> [2] *(this was only so that the generations of the children of Israel might be taught to know war, at least those who had not formerly known it).*

We have fought and won some battles that you won't have to fight again. We have conquered some territories that you will be able to possess without having to face what we have faced. But like this younger generation of Israelites, you will need to learn how to fight. There are unconquered territories that you will need to use your faith to obtain.

We are offering you our shoulders to stand upon. We are offering you our insight and experience. We are inviting you to join with us in our labors, rather than starting again from square one and having to relearn and recapture all that we have acquired.

Notwithstanding, you will still have your own battles to fight. You will have to face things that we have not. And like every generation that has gone before, you will find God to be faithful. You need to remember Deuteronomy 30:5,

> *"Then the LORD your God will bring you to the land which your fathers possessed, and you shall possess it. He will prosper you and multiply you more than your fathers."*

We are expecting you to excel and go beyond where we have been. Our hearts and our prayers are with you. Join us in the adventure of bringing a living Jesus to a dying world.

Stay the course. Be strong and very courageous. Our God will not leave you nor forsake you. His Word will be your light in the darkness, and His Spirit will strengthen and sustain you. And we will run this race with you.

TAKE ACTION

CHAPTER FIVE

Meditation

I will meditate on Your precepts, and contemplate Your ways. (Psalm 119:15)

Points to Ponder

1. Prayer is not just about God answering us; it is about us answering God.

2. The gifts, resources, influence, and creative insight required to reach this lost world do not reside in just one generation. God, in His wisdom, spread out what is needed across at least three generations.

3. The world is working hard to capture the hearts of our youth. If we don't engage the younger generations in Kingdom work, we may lose them.

4. The moment we stop changing, we start dying.

5. Engaging those from a younger generation can begin with something as simple as hosting a barbecue.

6. The younger generations need both the wisdom and the resources of those who are older if they are going to effectively reach the world for Christ.

7. As a young person, don't make the older folks do all the work when it comes to connecting. Take a "grayhead" to lunch and ask them some questions.

Our Final Authority—God's Word

The law of the LORD is perfect, converting the soul; the testimony of the LORD is sure, making wise the simple. (Psalm 19:7)

Psalm 89:1 (NASB)

I will sing of the _____ of the LORD

forever; _____ I will make

known Thy _____ with my mouth.

Philippians 3:17

Brethren, join in following my _____, and note

those who so walk, as you have us for a _____.

Psalm 71:18 (NLT)

Now that I am _____ and _____ , do not

abandon me, O God. Let me _____ your

power to this _____ , your

mighty miracles to all who _____ .

Galatians 4:19

My _____ , for whom

I _____ again until Christ is

_____ in you.

Deuteronomy 32:7

"Remember the days of old, _____

the years of _____ _____ .

Ask your _____ , and he will show you;

_____ , and they will tell you."

Deuteronomy 30:5

"Then the _____ will bring you to the

land which your _____ possessed, and you

shall _____ . He will prosper you and

_____ more than your fathers."

Application

What portions of the chapter stood out to you? Why? In what ways might they apply to you?

In what ways could you act upon and implement some of the principles brought out in this chapter? (Write down your thoughts and ideas. Even if they are rough and incomplete at this point, they will help you gain clarity and focus, and hopefully move you toward action.)

Group Discussion

Where there is no counsel, the people fall; but in the multitude of counselors there is safety. (Proverbs 11:14)

It is amazing how two people can read or hear the same words, yet their understanding of what was said can be vastly different. Take the time to let others express their thoughts and views. Good things can be gained by having a listening ear.

Always bring the discussion back to our final authority: God's Word.

Questions to Get You Started

Q. Do you think we will have a multigenerational church without purposely endeavoring to connect the generations (that it is just some sovereign work of God that doesn't depend upon us at all)?

Q. Do you think young people are genuinely searching to join and live for a cause that will make a difference?

Q. Maybe you don't know how to barbecue (or don't have the facilities or means to have a group of young people over for a meal). What CAN you do to engage with young people in a meaningful way (something that fits your personality and budget)?

Q. What would be a realistic amount of time to pray daily about connecting the generations?

Q. What would you say to someone who says they feel awkward about inviting an older person to lunch? (Do it as a group as opposed to going by yourself? Meet after or before a church service for coffee on the church campus?)

Q. As you move forward to do something to strengthen the generational connection in your church, should you keep the church leadership informed? (The answer is YES!)

Game Plan

I have kept my feet from every evil path so that I might obey your word. (Psalm 119:101 NIV)

Steps I will personally take to help connect the generations:

1. _____

2. _____

3. _____

Prayer

"Again I say to you that if two of you agree on earth concerning anything that they ask, it will be done for them by My Father in heaven." (Matthew 18:19)

If you are in a small group, take the time to pray for one another. Be specific concerning your requests. It might be good to let a different person lead in prayer for each request, while the others in the group lift their hearts in agreement.

Ask God for opportunities to sow into the life of someone from a different generation.

Pray a prayer to dedicate time and resources to connecting the generations.

Perhaps you know someone (from a younger generation) whom God would have you lift up in prayer on a regular basis. Seek God's wisdom and be obedient.

A WORD TO PASTORS AND CHURCH LEADERS

Many of the pastors and church leaders whom I have spoken to from around the globe feel an acute prompting to engage the younger generations, but they have expressed a general feeling of being overwhelmed by the magnitude of the task. In this final chapter, I want to share some thoughts that will help you get started in the work of reaching, raising up, and releasing the younger generations.

The first and most important thing to remember is that *we cannot accomplish this in our own strength*. Jesus said, *"I am the vine, you are the branches. He who abides in Me, and I in him, bears much fruit; for without Me you can do nothing"* (John 15:5).

We are co-laboring together with God, and as always, He is the one who does all the "heavy lifting." So from the outset, **YOU MUST SEED FOR CHANGE.** a simple prayer requesting His guidance, strength, and favor would certainly be in order. Then we can move forward with the confidence that His hand will direct us in our endeavors.

Here is a simple prayer that you might lift to the Father right now:

Dear heavenly Father, I thank You for all You have done in and through my life up to this point. I realize that one day I will exit this earthly life, and it is my desire to transfer all that You have given me to the younger generations. Help me to unselfishly pour my life into others. Guide me as I reach, raise up, and release young men and women into the glorious purposes of Your Kingdom. I ask that You help me to leave a legacy of faith that would continue on long after I am gone. In Jesus' name, amen.

GET IT INTO THE CHURCH'S BLOODSTREAM

As leaders of the church, it is our responsibility and privilege to download these truths into the hearts of our members—or, as I like to call it, "get it into the church's bloodstream."

BE AUTHENTIC. Paul's expressed desire for the Corinthian church was stated this way, *"Now I plead with you, brethren, by the name of our Lord Jesus Christ, that you all speak the same thing, and that there be no divisions among you, but that you be perfectly joined together in the same mind and in the same judgment"* (1 Corinthians 1:10). That is what we want when it comes to the generations working and serving together in God's House.

Following are some recommendations for accomplishing that goal:

1. Sow the Word

Anytime you want to bring about change in the church, you must *seed for change.* It is the Word of God that will ultimately change the hearts and mind-sets of our people, and that takes time.

Begin by having some informal meetings with your key leaders or staff members. Share your heart with them. Share from the Word and let them know what you want the future to look like concerning the generations. Do all you can to get them on board, igniting their hearts with the same fire that burns in yours.

Then, take the time to prepare and preach a series of messages on this subject to the congregation (use this book as an outline, if you like). Get the Word in people's hearts. Be patient but passionate. People will catch your enthusiasm and they will, in turn, begin sowing the same seeds of truth themselves, thus reinforcing the church's mission of bringing the generations together.

Small Groups

If your church already has small groups, introduce the teaching to them. Have them go through a series of teachings you have prepared, or have them read through this book together, using the TAKE ACTION section at the end of each chapter, which includes group discussion questions.

If you don't already have small groups in place, consider using your key leaders (after you have downloaded your heart into them) to teach a special month-long or six-week series of small group lessons either on your church campus or in people's homes (using the same materials).

If you prepare adequately and then pitch it right, you might be surprised at how many people sign up to both host and attend the meetings (especially if they know there is a beginning and an ending date).

The important thing is getting the Word into the hearts of the people. Once it is sown, it will do its work, even as the Scripture says, *"So the word of the Lord grew mightily and prevailed"* (Acts 19:20).

2. Personally Engage with Young People

It is important for you as a leader to do just that—lead, especially by example. Schedule time with young people from your church. If you have a youth pastor, share your vision for the generations with him or her, and ask the youth pastor to gather some of the youth to meet with you. Perhaps you could invite a group of them to your home. Get to know them. Share your heart with them, laugh with them, listen to them, pray with them. Get to know as many as you can by name.

My wife Janet hosted about a dozen young girls at our home once a week for several months. They watched a series of videos on sexual purity, had discussions, prayed, and ate lots of food. The girls usually ended up staying for hours just to talk and hang out. Friendships were forged both with my wife and one another. Several of those young women have become key leaders in our church.

Think about it, pray about it. How can you personally engage the younger generations? Others will observe you and will begin, both consciously and unconsciously, to do the same.

Thoughts to Consider

As you launch out and begin to build bridges into the lives of the younger generations, here are a few thoughts to consider:

a. <u>Be authentic</u>. Don't just share about all of the victories you've experienced in life and ministry. Honestly share about your setbacks and struggles as well. Young people are looking for truth—all of it. You can still be positive and faith-filled when you share about your mistakes and difficulties.

b. <u>Give them opportunities to spread their wings</u>. Let them share a thought at offering time. Let them preach during a service. Let them bring an exhortation during a service.

c. <u>Give them honest, encouraging feedback</u>. Let them know where they did well concerning the responsibility and authority you have given them. Make suggestions about where and how they might improve. Be a father to them.

3. Be Creative

Take time to pray and reflect on creative ways to connect the generations and get this message deeply embedded into the hearts of your church members. And it is important to realize that you won't have all the creative ideas yourself. Enlist the help of others—both young and old.

Perhaps get a group (representing at least three generations) together and give them the assignment to pray and think for a week, and then come up with a list of creative ways to implement your goals. Tell them that no idea will be too crazy or out of the box to consider.

When you meet again to share your thoughts, several things will become quite obvious. Like the fact that God is a God of variety. Or you may be somewhat out of touch with how young people think and relate. Or there may be a number of ways to accomplish a specific goal, each being equally valid. Or by the mere fact that you asked others for their input and help, you moved a long way forward in cementing relationships and connecting people of different generations.

A Few Things That Have Been Done

Just to help further kick-start the process, here is a list of a few things that have been done by either myself or others. (Feel free to implement any that appeal to you, and by all means please add to the list some ideas of your own.)

1. Meet one morning a week at a local coffee shop with a group of young people for a short Bible study.

2. Make a series of five-minute videos. Older folks can share their most important life lesson with young people, and young people can share some words to honor their elders. The older people's videos can be shared periodically during youth meetings, and the young people's videos can be shared before the Sunday morning message.

3. Take younger people out regularly to golf, fish, or whatever you do for recreation.

4. Host dinners with a mixture of old and young people, creating an environment that is fun and conducive to connection.

5. Send younger and older volunteers together on short-term mission trips.

6. Have a young couple or group of young people invite an older couple out to dinner, and have some questions ready (about life, marriage, ministry, etc.).

7. Get the youth band in your church to participate monthly or bimonthly by leading worship in the regular services.

8. Have some of your key young people sit in on church financial meetings. If they are going to work alongside you and one day inherit the work to carry on, they need insight on how things work financially.

9. Get things paid off so the upcoming generations can focus on the harvest field, rather than having to deal with inherited unpaid debt.

10. Make sure that key young people are in front of the congregation regularly, either preaching, receiving the offering, or making the transition between different elements of the service.

11. Have regular meetings with young and older key leaders to discuss the weekend services. How can they be made better? What technology would help us? Would short dramas help? What needs to be reassessed? Are we doing things because of a tradition that no longer has meaning?

12. Have successful businesspeople set up mentoring classes or programs for young people to help them succeed in life and business.

13. Set up an intern program whereby young people who feel called to ministry can serve alongside others who have experience in ministry.

14. Plan some fun teamwork days where you go to an obstacle course or do something that requires teamwork between the young and old in order to succeed.

Finally, may we who are older remember that, most generally, we were young men and women when we started in ministry.

God somehow got us through all of our rough patches, and He continues to use us until this present hour. His Church is not as fragile as some would make it out to be.

The same God who saw us through and sustained the work will continue to do so, as He uses both young and old hands, and burning hearts from all generations.

A Final Picture to Consider

15 When the Philistines were at war again with Israel, David and his servants with him went down and fought against the Philistines; and David grew faint. 16 Then Ishbi-Benob, who was one of the sons of the giant, the weight of whose bronze spear was three hundred shekels, who was bearing a new sword, thought he could kill David. 17 But Abishai the son of Zeruiah came to his aid, and struck the Philistine and killed him. Then the men of David swore to him, saying, "You shall go out no more with us to battle, lest you quench the lamp of Israel."

18 Now it happened afterward that there was again a battle with the Philistines at Gob. Then Sibbechai the Hushathite killed Saph, who was one of the sons of the giant. 19 Again there was war at Gob with the Philistines, where Elhanan the son of Jaare-Oregim the Bethlehemite killed the brother of Goliath the Gittite, the shaft of whose spear was like a weaver's beam.

20 Yet again there was war at Gath, where there was a man of great stature, who had six fingers on each hand and six toes on each foot, twenty-four in number; and he also was born to the giant. ²¹ *So when he defied Israel, Jonathan the son of Shimea, David's brother, killed him.*

²² *These four were born to the giant in Gath, and fell by the hand of David and by the hand of his servants.* (2 Samuel 21:15-22)

This story takes place during the later years of David's reign. He had previously killed Goliath and routed the Philistine army, but he is in a different season of life now. He can no longer do all that he once did, nor is he called to do it all.

David's heart is worthy of admiration. He was with his soldiers on the battlefield. He still had the heart to do the "hard yards" and the "heavy lifting," but the fact was he could no longer carry on as he once had. The scene has radically changed from David the young giant killer to an older David almost being killed by a giant.

A Few Points for Contemplation

1. David has reached a season of transition in his life and ministry, as do all of God's servants. He navigated it well. May we do the same.

2. The attitude of the young warriors was one of absolute respect and honor. They realized David's value as a seasoned leader— both to them and to all of Israel—and they sought to protect him (v. 17).

3. The younger soldiers began killing giants just as David once had.

4. Their victories were attributed to David (v. 22).

I would strongly urge every leader to take some time to meditate on this story. Many of us are either in or entering into transitional times in our lives and ministries, and it is imperative that we transition well.

There will always be people who say, "David, no one kills giants like you do. No one handles that sling and sends out the Word like you do. We know you want to release these young men and women, but we like it when you're the one killing giants! We don't like it when you're not in the forefront."

If you yield to the pressure of these well-meaning folks, they will get you killed! More giants will be slain by working with and empowering the younger generations, and more territories will be won.

Navigating Well

A common story is told of a man who was looking for a new captain to pilot his riverboat up a treacherous stretch of river filled with hidden sandbars. The owner of the boat was interviewing a man whom many claimed was the best captain on the river. "So, you're the best captain on this river, are you? Why is that? Do you know where all the dangerous sandbars are?"

"No," the man replied, "but I know where they ain't!"

Just as there are different stretches of river that need to be navigated, there are different seasons of life and ministry that need to be navigated. Some navigate those seasons well, while others do not.

We need to be like the sons of Issachar...

> *The sons of Issachar who had understanding of*
> *the times, to know what Israel ought to do...*
> (1 Chronicles 12:32)

If you are in a season of change, may God grant you the wisdom and the grace to transition well. In this time of life when you are the most valuable because of your gifting, wisdom, and experience, may you be like the sons of Issachar who knew what to do. My prayer is that the thoughts contained in this book will help you successfully reach, raise up, and release the generations—no matter what season you may be in.

TAKE ACTION

CHAPTER SIX

Meditation

My eyes are awake through the night watches, that I may meditate on Your word. (Psalm 119:148)

Points to Ponder

1. We cannot successfully reach, raise up, and release the younger generations in our own strength and ability. We must rely on God.

2. Anytime you want to bring about change in the church, you must seed for change. Passionately and patiently share the truths of God's Word concerning the generations working together.

3. Spend time personally with groups of young people from your church. Get to know them and let them get to know you.

4. Share from your own life experience with young people, being honest about your setbacks and struggles, as well as your victories.

5. Give young people opportunities to participate in important aspects of your church services (and make sure to give them honest and helpful feedback so they can improve).

6. Perhaps get a small group together, representing all three generations, to come up with some creative ideas for connecting the generations in your church.

Our Final Authority—God's Word

"Heaven and earth will pass away, but My words will by no means pass away." (Matthew 24:35)

John 15:5

> *"I am the _____, you are the _____.*
>
> *He who abides in Me, and _____,*
>
> *bears much fruit; for _____ you can do*
>
> *_____."*

1 Corinthians 1:10

"Now I plead with you, brethren, by the _____ of

our _____ , that you all

_____ the _____,

and that there be no _____ among you, but that

you be _____ together in the

same _____ and in the same _____."

Acts 19:20

"So the _____ of the Lord _____

and _____."

Application

What portions of the chapter stood out to you? Why? In what ways might they apply to you?

In what ways could you act upon and implement some of the principles brought out in this chapter? (Write down your thoughts and ideas. Even if they are rough and incomplete at this point, they will help you gain clarity and focus, and hopefully move you toward action.)

_____

_____

_____

_____

_____

_____

_____

_____

_____

_____

_____

_____

_____

_____

_____

_____

_____

Group Discussion

Now the apostles and elders came together to consider this matter.
(Acts 15:6)

Do your best to draw others into the conversation. A simple question of "What do you think about the ideas presented in this chapter?" or "What stood out to you the most about this chapter?", when addressed to even the most reserved member of the group, may spark some lively and valuable conversation.

Questions to Get You Started

Q. Why is it important to spend time patiently planting seeds for change? Shouldn't everyone just immediately get on board and do what the leader says?

Q. How important is it to have the "blessing" from your church leadership before you start meeting with young people (or anyone, for that matter) in the pursuit of creating a multigenerational church? (Most would just call this being submitted to authority [Hebrews 13:17].)

Q. What ways might you go about engaging other church members to get them actively on board and participating as you endeavor to reach, raise up, and release the younger generations?

Q. How can you keep the older members in your church from being discouraged or feeling left out as you focus on connecting with the youth?

Game Plan

[47] *"Whoever comes to Me, and hears My sayings and does them, I will show you whom he is like:* [48] *He is like a man building a house, who dug deep and laid the foundation on the rock. And when the flood arose, the stream beat vehemently against that house, and could not shake it, for it was founded on the rock."* (Luke 6:47-48)

Steps I will personally take to help connect the generations:

1. _____

2. _____

3. _____

Prayer

Be anxious for nothing, but in everything by prayer and supplication, with thanksgiving, let your requests be made known to God. (Philippians 4:6)

Perhaps it would be in order to worship the Lord for a few minutes, and then just sit quietly as you digest the things you have read and discussed in this chapter. You may find the Holy Spirit impressing upon your heart or speaking to you about the season of life and ministry you are in, or about your role in having a multigenerational church.

Expect God to guide you. Listen for that "still, small voice" and always be quick to obey His Word.

ABOUT THE AUTHOR

Bayless Conley is the lead pastor of Cottonwood Church in Orange County, California, and the Bible teacher on the global television outreach *Answers with Bayless Conley*. Bayless is known for his clear teaching of the truths of God's Word, and the practical application of those truths to life.

Born and raised in Southern California, Bayless was drawn into a life of drug and alcohol abuse as a teen, which ultimately led him on an intense pursuit to find meaning in life. It was on that journey that he discovered the grace and love of Jesus Christ through the testimony of a 12-year-old boy.

Bayless' unique background and remarkable story have enabled him to reach a diverse global audience with the life-transforming message of the Gospel. And today, *Answers with Bayless Conley* is translated into numerous languages, reaching the nations of the world.

Bayless and his wife Janet have been married since 1982. They are the parents of three grown children and the fun-loving grandparents of two. Bayless and Janet are passionate in their pursuit of God, life, and family.

Bayless is the author of numerous books and booklets, including *Cast Down, But Not Destroyed*; *Footprints of Faith*; *How to Pray*; *Turning Mistakes into Miracles*; *Understanding Salvation*; *The Infilling of the Holy Spirit*; *Where Is God When Hard Times Hit?*; *There Is Always Hope*; and a 365-day devotional called *Answers for Each Day*.